MW00985650

HIDDEN GOD

HIDDEN GOD

LADISLAUS BOROS

Translated by
Erika Young

A Continuum Book
THE SEABURY PRESS · NEW YORK

THE SEABURY PRESS
815 Second Avenue, New York 10017

Published originally under the title *Der gute Mensch und sein
Gott*, © Walter-Verlag A.G. Olten 1971
English translation © Search Press Limited, 1973
ISBN: 0-8164-1042-9
Library of Congress Catalog Card Number: 72-3939
Printed in the United States of America

Contents

FOREWORD   7

1. Undiscovered Man   11
2. Threatened Man   25
3. Silent Man   42
4. Friendly Man   56
5. Helpful Man   69
6. Protected Man   85
7. Happy Man   101
8. Seeking Man   116

Foreword

"THEY have taken away my Lord, and I do not know where they have laid him" (John 20. 13). This book does not pretend to answer this poignant lament of our age of seeking, but it does try to help man rediscover God—who is "closer to him than his own heart".[1]

It is perhaps easier to say what this book is not than to summarize its content. It is not another book about God's absence, which does not mean that it would not be meaningful to work out a theology of the distance of God,[2] to confront man the seeker with a greater God than he has so far known,[3] and to show him the meaning of his own loneliness: "There is no way out for true misery. The true misery of the miserable can only find an outlet in God."[4]

It would be equally valuable to follow through the experience of God's distance to its uttermost limit, and to try to understand belief from the basis of the experience behind the following words: "God is dead. God has died of his compassion for men."[5]

Finally one must not overlook the human measure of the new

1. "Deus interior intimo meo", Augustine. *Confessions* (III. 6; 11). See also *Dictionnaire de la Spiritualité* (Vol. 1, especially col. 437; Paris, 1937). This entry (*Ame*) is a valuable source of insights into the relationship of the soul to God.

2. See L. Boros, "*Ich glaube, hilf meinem Unglauben!*" *Reflexionen über die dialektische Struktur des ungläubigen Glaubens* (Der grosse Entschluss, July/August–September, 1961, p. 444 f. and 500 ff.).

3. E. Przywara used Augustine's words "Deus semper maior" to characterize Ignatian spirituality. See *Deus semper maior. Theologie der Exerzitien* (Freiburg im Breisgau, 1938–40).

4. Georges Bernanos, Letters, in *Oeuvres complètes* (Paris, 1950).

5. Nietzsche, *Also sprach Zarathustra* (*Thus spake Zarathustra*).

"negative" theology, which attempts to plumb the depths of human need. Its intellectual roots are in the pain of our own time. It is human thinking constantly applied to the essence of intense human care and suffering, responsibility and despair. The new theologians have themselves known the wretchedness of human existence, and in the light of their experience want to help their friends through times of failure and discouragement. Their writings show that they have truly known heaviness of soul and the weight of responsibility. They are well aware that words of freedom can be spoken only by those who have themselves taken up the Cross, and have carried it right into the fearful moment expressed in the words: "My God, my God, why hast thou forsaken me?" (Mt. 27. 46). The "theology of the Cross" arises where man's thinking about God causes him to save his brother from ultimate despair, and embrace him with kindness and friendship.[6] There is no room here for righteousness and accusation,[7] but only for pity and compassion. These impulses have led to the development of a new, prophetically strong, theology of brotherly presence, and to a way of thinking about God that derives from the particular grace of the moment.

But this book will not attempt these paths. It will speak of the *nearness* of God, of the luminance of his presence, which is the source of peace and joy. It will try to indicate God's presence in the world—a presence which, as Paul says, is plain to men because God has revealed himself in the things that he has made (Rom. 1. 19–20). For thousands of years religion and theology have attempted to express

6. The "new theologians" are discussed in more detail in my article, "Theologische Erfahrungen einer Vortragsreise in Deutschland" in *Orientierung, 29, 6,* March 31st 1965, pp. 61–3.

7. Unfortunately there is a great deal of accusation in the words of certain once open-minded philosophers and theologians, like Maritain, *Le Paysan de la Garonne* (Paris, 1966; Eng. trans. *The Peasant of the Garonne*, London, 1967), or D. von Hildebrand, *Das trojanische Pferd in der Stadt Gottes* (Stein am Rhein, 1968). It is not for us to pass judgment on the writings and ideas of these distinguished people. On the other hand it is permissible to feel somewhat estranged, and rather sad.

in human concepts the mystery of the glory of God illuminating the human spirit. But with little success.[8] They have been able to give us only the remotest inkling of the mystery. What lies closest is most difficult to grasp; what is nearest is most unclear; what is simplest is most difficult to say. Man needs great stillness to feel the true presence of Him who is "the stillest of all"—to whom we give the name God.

Behind every book is a wealth of personal experience. *"Habent sua fata libelli."* This book was written during months of inner and outer withdrawal at a place on the edge of the Irish sea. For the writer it was a time set apart. He wanted to share his joy with others, with friends in whom he had recently sensed an encroaching sadness. The best form of consolation for others was—he thought—to have greater joy oneself, and to think joyfully for others. Men have never rejoiced enough. Their life has not sufficiently turned into "joyful tidings". It is difficult to live a life of joy simply because silence and stillness are themselves so difficult.

This then is a book that is "quiet" in expression, ideas and style; one that coerces no one, hurts no one, and in general refrains from concrete objectives. The greatest events take place not in our noisiest but in our stillest hours.

8. See, on "glory", the second volume of Hans Urs von Balthasar's *Herrlichkeit, eine theologische Ästhetik*, Vol. 2, *Fächer der Stile* (Einsiedeln, 1962). Balthasar analyses the ideas of the following thinkers: Irenaeus, Augustine, Dionysius, Anselm, Bonaventure, Dante, John of the Cross, Pascal, Hamann, Soloviev, Hopkins and Péguy. One can see from the work of these men what efforts it has meant for the human spirit to encompass God's glory in its own realm.

1. Undiscovered Man

MAN is still undiscovered and unexhausted. We can discover his secret only fragmentarily. Even such an attempt as this book is presumption, and must be undertaken in modesty and humility.

This book was originally entitled "Being and Transcendence: The Religious and Philosophical Foundations of a Christian Anthropology". Although this is an exact description of the book's contents, as a title it might seem unduly trying to the reader's patience. Nevertheless it will serve to introduce the first of our meditations.

The meaning and intention of the book are expressed in the six words of this original title. An understanding of these six concepts is a prerequisite for further examination of the subject. Hurried thinking does not help one to get to the essence of the matter. A poet might be able to speak simply yet profoundly of the good man and his God: the poet Mörike, perhaps, of whom it was said: "Mörike takes a handful of earth, shapes it a little, and soon a small bird flies away."[1] Unfortunately our way is harder.

The first of the six concepts is:

Being

This word is intended to describe *man as a whole*, in his "indivisibility". In using it to indicate the direction I mean to take, I also show that I want to construct a philosophy that does not try to explain man by means of his different parts, functions and qualities, but concentrates on his uniqueness and inalienable destiny. I

---

1. See W. Weber's interpretation of Mörike's poem, "Der Gärtner", in his *Tagebuch eines Lesers* (Olten, 1965), pp. 59–65.

shall consider man as he presents himself: in his once-and-for-all "presence" in the world.[2] But this cannot be done hastily. We must try to understand the essence of what is presented, and the way in which it is done. This means that seeing must become understanding, as happens in the courtesy of personal encounter, and the receptiveness of listening. We must get rid of the harmful kind of subjectivity composed of impatience, curiosity and ready-made ideas.

"Being" also means what is *not* directly accessible. Of course human life also contains the everyday things that go with the person. But these are not what a man understands by his "life".[3] Man feels that this uniqueness of life, which he calls "being", is wholly good. It consists of moments of awareness and wonder, when he is confronted by the most basic questions. He begins to understand the real meaning of "being" in such moments of heightened awareness, and tries to give shape to his ideas. "Abstraction", a mode of thought which no philosophy aiming at universal meaning can afford to do without, consists precisely in not trying to understand man in general terms, that is, in not explaining him in terms of his functions and reactions. The philosophy of "being" is an attempt to elucidate the uniqueness and unchangeability of individual destiny.

But in order to state the meaning of "being" validly, one must create the language in which to express what one has understood. "Being" as heightened existence seen in its totality and uniqueness is found where man is "central"—in that sphere, therefore, where his spiritual, intellectual and physical elements are indissolubly linked. But this is precisely where images are formed. Thus the truest and wisest things about human life can normally only be expressed in images.

One example will make this clear. The Ash Wednesday liturgy at

2. For a fuller explanation of "being" see the work of Heidegger. Individual citations are best found in H. Feick, *Index zu Heideggers "Sein und Zeit"* (Tübingen, 1968; especially under the headings *Da* (p. 11), *Sein des Da* (p. 12) and *Dasein* (pp. 12–15)).

3. See J. Durandeaux, *L'Eternité dans la vie quotidienne* (Bruges, 1968), especially pp. 175–217).

one point calls on man to reflect about himself, and has this to say about human life: "Remember, man, that you are dust." The image of "dust" refers to the whole of man—not only his body but his spiritual soul. The immediate meaning is that man is dedicated to death, is moving towards dissolution. But the symbolism goes deeper: Man has no continuance, no resting place, he can be found everywhere and yet is nowhere truly at home. Thus one can see how a simple image can slowly change into a statement about life itself.[4] And furthermore it is impossible to take an image to pieces, because images do not try to solve problems, only to illumine mystery.[5]

Understanding about being means breaking with all one's preconceptions. In order to be able to see lines that are forever converging but never touching, one must have the courage to face mystery and the strength of recognition; one needs a philosophy that is oriented to mystery. There must be continuous preoccupation with even the most unimportant aspects of life; a grasping hold of human reality in the knowledge that it is ultimately beyond our grasp.[6]

Thus we come to the second concept.

Transcendence

The experience of these "high points of life"[7] out of which true being grows takes place in circumstances that I would call

4. For further reference, see my article "Les Catégories de la Temporalité chez Saint Augustine", in *Archives de Philosophie*, July–September 1968, pp. 323–85.

5. The distinction between "problem" and "mystery" was made by G. Marcel. See R. Troisfontaine's *De L'Existence à L'Etre: La Philosophie de Gabriel Marcel* (Louvain & Paris, 1953). See especially, vol. 1, pp. 263–84.

6. Cf. E. Przywara, *Gott. Fünf Vorträge über das religionsphilosophische Problem*; new edition in *Religionsphilosopsische Schriften* (Einsiedeln, 1962).

7. Here we must make a clear distinction between the concept "salvation" and Jaspers' concept of a "border situation". The distinction is accurately described in X. Tilliette's *Philosophes contemporains* (Paris, 1962), pp. 87–110.

"openness". What is meant by this is best shown in the following account by Gertrud the Great:

"One day, between Easter and Ascension, before Prime, I went into the courtyard, sat down beside the fish pond, and gazed at the loveliness of the place where I was. The clarity of the flowing waters, the green of the surrounding trees, the free flight of the birds and especially the doves, but above all the heavenly quiet, filled me with well-being. I began to wonder what more could be added to complete my joy. I thought to myself that I needed a friend, someone well-known to me, affectionate and sympathetic, to sweeten my loneliness. Thereupon you, my God, cause of indescribable bliss, led my thoughts to yourself, and without doubt it was you yourself who guided them. You showed me how my heart could be a pleasant dwelling place for you. In return I must, as this water reminds me, direct the flow of grace in proper, inexhaustible gratitude back to yourself. I must, like these trees, flower in the greenness of good works, increase in strength and unfold in good deeds. I must, like the doves, look on the things of earth from above, and lift myself in unfettered flight to the things of heaven, where my soul, freed from the thoughts and cares of the world, can be totally concentrated on you. Thus my heart will become a dwelling place for you that is more precious than any loveliness."[8]

8. Gertrud the Great (1256–1302), "Gesandter der göttlichen Liebe" III/3, quoted in G. Gieraths, *Abgrund des Lichtes, Texte deutscher Mystik* (Einsiedeln, 1964), pp. 78–9. I should like to quote two further passages here which express the same view: 'In my early days it once happened that I went into choir on St Agnes' Day, just after the Convent lunch. I was on my own and stood in the low stall on the right-hand side of the choir. And suddenly a curiously troubled feeling of deep suffering came upon me. And as I stood there inconsolable, and no one was with me, my soul was carried away, in the body or outside the body. Then I saw and heard what no tongue can utter. It was without kind or form, yet contained within itself every kind and form of joy. The heart was hungry and yet satisfied, the senses joyful and happy. My wishes had been met, my desire was stilled. I did nothing but stare into the bright light in which I forgot myself and everything else. I did not know whether it was day or night ... Then I said: If this is not the kingdom of heaven, then I do not know what the kingdom of heaven is. For all the suffering that can be expressed in words cannot earn joy for him who is destined

First there must be a deep penetration into the world itself, which is seen as something clear and light. But the peace that exists between man and the world is disturbed by an increasing longing for "still more". What has been achieved so far is not enough. The dynamism of life drives man forward to new revelations. Suddenly the figure of the friend appears. Life becomes "life with him". Stimulated by this positive experience, longing increases still further. Not even eternal being can lessen the violence of the ever heightening tension. When the image of an eternal transcendental being appears to the onlooker, he seizes hold of it with intuitive immediacy. But then he tries to enclose the infinite within his own finitude. And in so doing returns to the concrete form of things. Now, however, he is aware of a changed world, a new clarity, an existential transparency. The tangible things of the world point to the intangible, the finite to the infinite. What ultimately remains to man are only his own desires—a longing to "flow", to "flower", to "float upwards". These are finite images of the infinite, measurable activities directed towards the immeasurable, relative being towards Absolute. They are adoration of the mystery in the insignificant forms of the world, the pull towards eternity within the limited scope of life upon earth. Since this "pull" or tension is in every sense "intangible", it

---

to possess it eternally. This intoxication lasted for an hour or half an hour. And when I came once more to myself, it was as if I had come from another world. This taste of heaven remained with me for a long time and gave me a heavenly longing for God" (H. Seuse, *ibid.*, p. 104). "I could in no way recognise the shape of the light, just as I cannot fully look on the shape of the sun. In this light I sometimes, though not often, see another light that is described to me as the 'living light'. When and in what manner I saw it, I cannot say. But as long as I see it, all sadness and fear are taken away from me . . . And what I see and grasp in this vision fills my soul as from a fountain that remains full and inexhaustible . . . I see it as though I see the heavens in a light cloud, without stars. There I see what I usually say and what I answer when I am asked about the brilliance of this 'living light'." (Hildegard von Bingen, *Brief an Gilbert von Gembloux, ibid*, pp. 98–9).

projects itself into earthly images, in order to enter into human consciousness.

What is the meaning of the pull towards the eternal? Central to the experience described above is the awareness—"It was you, my God, who led my thoughts to yourself, and without doubt it was you yourself who guided them." Man feels this pull as the effect upon him of the Absolute. The infinite itself is seen as source, end, and goal of the flow of life. Thus what is unreachable grows near, and takes root within man. In its transcendence it becomes immanent. Its presence is made manifest in the way man moves, is driven and pulled. Hence the Absolute does not, on the one hand, belong to life, but on the other it creates the very essence of it. The essential meaning of human life is this: The unreachable is what men need and long for. The Absolute that is far away is at the same time profoundly near.[9] This ontological fact of life lies at the root of every other human awareness and experience, and deeply affects them from the start.[10]

We are now in possession of the concepts by means of which the philosophies of transcendence, all of them versions of a "philosophy of longing", attempt to explain God's presence in every appearance of human life.[11] Man is driven by an urge towards transcendence, an

9. At this point I refer the reader to E. Przywara's short formula of the analogy ("Gott-in-und-über") as expounded in his work, *Analogia Entis* (Munich, 1932; new edition, vol. 3 of E. Przywara's writings, 1962).

10. I should like to refer here to K. Rahner's use of the word "existential" in theological discussion. The "existential" inescapably precedes and conditions man's free action. Only on this basis of ontological reality can the "actual" (*das Existentielle*—what arises from man's free action) be thinkable at all. Thus the "existential" precedes personal decision. A more detailed exposition can be found in K. Rahner's *Schriften zur Theologie I* (Einsiedeln, 1954); see pp. 96 ff., 99 ff., 250 ff., 328; and in vol. 2, pp. 68 and 252); Eng. trans.: *Theological Investigations*, vol. I). Since, according to Heidegger, there are different forms of existentiality (see H. Feick, *Index zu Heideggers "Sein und Zeit"*, Tübingen, 1968. Cf. "existential", p. 26, and "existentiell-existential", pp. 26–7). I prefer to speak here of an "existential basis").

11. My short essay on the "transcendental method" appeared under the

urge that is deliberately geared to the heightened moment of life, but whose real content remains hidden in a "light-shadowy darkness".[12]

Man looks for forms of words, meaning, concepts and above all images that will give it conscious expression. The urge for understanding is called the *projective function* of the life force. It utters itself in religion. And so we come to the third point to help us formulate more exactly our present intention.

The Philosophy of Religion

This is where man's transcendental experience returns to its own proper source, in the form of reflection upon that experience. It takes place in the dialectical process.[13]

First: The human mind projects its experience of Unconditioned Being into the world of the accessible, imaginable and sayable. The

---

title "Neuvollzug der Metaphysik" in *Orientierung*, vol. 24. 3, in February 15th 1960, pp. 34 f. The transcendental method consists essentially of a release of the basic presuppositions that every self-expression contains, in an unreflective and undefined form. I should like to draw attention here to O. Muck's *Die transzendentale Methode in der scholastischen Philosophie der Gegenwart* (Innsbruck, 1964). A good summary is also found in E. Coreth's *Metaphysik. Eine methodisch-systematische Grundlegung* (Innsbruck, 1961), especially pp. 69 ff. See also *Metaphysik als Aufgabe* (Innsbruck, 1958). I have listed the most important thinkers of the modern transcendental method in note 16 of my *Mysterium Mortis* (London, 1968). In another context, but completely appropriate to the matter under discussion, H. Urs von Balthasar described the view of the "transcendental method" thinkers in *Herrlichkeit* III/2, Part 1 (Einsiedeln, 1967), pp. 41–3.

12. See Dionysius the pseudo-Areopagite, *De Divinis Nominibus* (l. 1) and the commentary by E. Pryzywara, *Gott* (Cologne & Munich, 1926), pp. 22–3; or in the new edition, *Religionsphilosophische Schriften* (Einsiedeln, 1926), vol. 2, p. 255. See also J. Vanneste, *Le Mystère de Dieu. Essai sur la Structure rationelle de la Doctrine mystique du Pseudo-Denys L'Aréopagite* (Bruges, 1959).

13. What is being analysed here is not the so-called "fides quae creditur" (the content of faith) but the "fides qua creditur" (the act of faith itself).

Absolute is clothed in human words, and gives concrete expression to man's longing. But the essence of the Absolute, the goal towards which the human mind is striving, constantly eludes man and disappears in a vague mist.[14]

After the experience of transcendence—such as has been described in the account of Gertrud the Great quoted above—the projective function of the life force can begin to express itself in concrete form, behaviour and language. It is from this that religion springs. In an historical process—in which non-reflective norms of action, unarticulated descriptions and decisions about the divine are made— the deliberate movement of being towards the Absolute grows into "objective faith". The task and function of this faith is to direct man's gaze unwaveringly towards God. Thus the human mind attempts a task which, at first sight, seems useless, indeed impossible: the concrete and systematic realization of subjective experience.[15] But

14. G. Siewerth treats the fundamental two-sidedness of man's experience of being with impressive intellectual rigour in *Das Sein als Gleichnis Gottes*. God approaches the human spirit in every spiritual act directed towards himself, and at the same time withdraws into a transcendental apartness. The God-directedness of the human soul takes place in an "approach through distance". Every transcendental step widens still further the abyss of difference. This basic structure of "nearness to God through distance from him" in the human soul is the metaphysical presupposition for the dialectic of faith that I try to describe here.

15. I am not suggesting a "purely functional explanation of the institution" in the manner of A. Gehlen. Gehlen gives the following examples: "The formless longing of man acquires its form in marriage, particularly in monogamy. This saves man from the creative experience of continually refashioning the marriage experience and at every stage in life having to look anew for a suitable partner. The tie of convention protects him from endless decision-making, which uses up his strength in vain and makes him no longer fully capable of reaching his goal—the conquest of nature. "For Gehlen, marriage and convention are only rules for the proper ordering of society. They could be quite different, but can never be wholly absent if man wants to survive. It is the same with man's relation towards God, worship and the Church. These save him from the search for personal religious experience, which is already in one form or another contained in them. In this way the relationship of the

this realization of life's direction is only the outer shell of the real movement of faith.

In the last analysis man does not believe in his own statements about God. He believes in God himself, quite simply because God is his God and leads his thoughts towards a loving union (*credere Deum, credere Deo, credere in Deum*).[16] Faith rests in itself, is its own cause, cannot be explained by formulas, concepts, modes of behaviour, proofs. These are projections that must always be transcended. They are only introductions to the act of faith. Man's mind, indeed the collective mind of the human race, must work without ceasing upon these "statements", "objectivisations" and "systems" of religion. Thus there develops a rich and varied body of ideas through which the individual can experience the real reasons for his existence.[17]

---

individual to the Absolute is duly ordered, and he does not waste in restless religious searching the energies that he so greatly needs in the life struggle." See M. Müller, "Die Person und die Institutionen", in *Orientierung*, vol. 127, no. 19, October 15th 1963, pp. 211 ff; and no. 20, October 31st 1963, pp. 227 f. We can see the correctness of Gehlen's view, that community living has the enormously important function of saving the individual from having to find his own form of life, yet institutions must not exclusively be seen from the purely functional aspect of organs of administration. It is precisely the analysis of historical life that enables us to find the super-factual within the factual.

16. "Credere Deum, Deo, in Deum" is a classical formulation to clarify the theological act of faith in the light of the following structure—God as content (*Deum*), as witness (*Deo*) and as goal (*in deum*) of each act of faith. See also J. B. Metz, "Credere Deum, Deo, in Deum" (*Lexikon für Theologie und Kirche* (Freiburg, 1959), vol. 3, cols 86–8).

17. The dialectic between the intention of faith and the statement of belief was very ably discussed by H. Duméry (in *La Foi n'est pas un cri*) as early as 1957. One year later the book was put on the Index. Two years later Duméry brought out a second and considerably enlarged edition (Paris, 1959) containing certain far-reaching alterations. This edition was not put on the Index and may be recommended to intelligent Christians. Duméry's basic thesis may be evaluated positively—namely that faith is no "cry", and no vague longing for the Absolute. It is the acceptance of an historical tradition. It encloses

Second: All too often it happens that the ideas intended as aids for the mind become goals in themselves, and the act of faith is swallowed up in religious formulas which then no longer fulfil their purpose of opening the way to a higher sphere. Thus a real contradiction arises. On the one hand the transcendental nature of being has to be made concrete by means of representational ideas; but on the other it erects, in the course of this process, an opaque wall between itself and the Absolute, and builds barriers across the path along which it is moving. When this happens faith must sound out its own work and deny its own projections. In the course of this denial clarity of vision returns, and man is made ready to move once more in the direction of God. Thus the denial of faith (often superficially described as atheism) is part of the essential structure of faith itself. Denial of faith is in no sense a "perverse malformation of the spirit" but something that is always present in the life of the believer, and must always be overcome. A conscious, mature and honestly lived faith will never be unsympathetic to non-belief which it sees not as something totally other, but as a constituent part of its own search for God.[18]

Third: The tension between projection of faith and denial of faith finally leads to the transcendence of faith. As the individual experiences the limitations of religious concepts, demands, categories, modes of behaviour and practices, he gathers together the sum total of his faith projections in order to move with even greater intensity towards the Absolute. Thus God becomes once more

---

necessary institutions and statements within itself and is thereby brought to completion. Religious experience has objective forms. This is the paradox of a positive religion, that it takes up the most personal element of our relationship with God and turns it into an historical fact. Using the phenomenological method, Duméry showed that institutions were of the essence of faith. Individual points in the book may still give rise to justified criticism, but in my view, the basic thesis applies aptly to the structure of faith.

18. For a more detailed treatment, see my article, "Ich glaube, hilf meinem Unglauben" (*Der grosse Entschluss*, vol. 16, September 1961, part 2, p. 502).

present to the believer in the inner tension of faith, in the sphere of that which can only be grasped through being objectified, but which all the same is totally transcended. The task of the philosophy of religion,[19] therefore, is this: By means of intellectual analysis to reduce all religious objectivizations to their basic intention, and thus accurately to test the validity and usefulness of all individual concretizations.

Establishing the Argument

We are concerned here with referring human life back to its ultimate cause—to that which is not caused by anything else but exists in and of itself; to the uncaused cause that is the cause of all other causes. Subjectively it is a matter of the ultimate proof of the Absolute. But objectively it concerns that Reality which is independent of ourselves and is freely conveyed to us in the circumstances of our attraction towards it. It is a matter of illumination overwhelming man's senses, understanding and will to such an extent that he can no longer escape from the absolute cause of being. It is only by means of such a transformation of life into vision that we can have true proof of the Absolute, and therefore also true reasons for our own existence. Thus what is required here—being and event in one —pierces man "to the division of soul and spirit, of joints and marrow" (Hebr. 4. 12). The Absolute must be freely revealed within human experience. God manifesting himself as light must encompass man's senses. This fundamental proof of God's presence is referred to in the Bible as "glory" (*doxa*). It is the appearance of the Absolute within creation (*schechina*), the force and power of the felt nearness of God (*kabod*), which draws men to itself by its beauty (*chesed* and *chen*). Man therefore is overwhelmed by absolute beauty.

19. This task (of the philosophy of religion) has been very carefully dealt with in the writings of H. Duméry. See also a more fundamental treatment of the works of Duméry up to that time in my article, *Entschematisiertes Christentum* (*Orientierung*, vol. 22, No. 14/15, July 31st 1958, pp. 152 ff and no. 16, August 31st 1958, pp. 169 ff).

We should like to insert into our philosophy this biblical concept in the fullness of its meaning. We are convinced that human existence can ultimately only be explained in the light of the experience of the glory of God.[20] Beauty is in the biblical and also in the philosophical sense the foundation of human existence and also its last word—the word which turns into the silence of man before the mystery.

Man's encounter with God is shown in the Bible in various ways. Face to face with God's glory, Moses "made haste to bow his head towards the earth" (Ex. 34. 8); Elijah "wrapped his face in his mantle" (1 Kings 19. 13); Isiah believed himself to be "lost" (Is. 6. 5); Ezekiel writes: "I fell upon my face" (Ez. 1. 28); Daniel says: "My spirit within me was anxious and the visions of my head alarmed me" (Dan. 7. 15); and "When I heard the sound of his words, I fell on my face in a deep sleep with my face to the ground" (Dan. 10. 9); the Apostles "were exceedingly afraid" (Mark 9. 6); "were heavy with sleep" (Luke 9. 32); "were filled with awe" (Mt. 17. 16). "Suddenly a light from heaven flashed about" Paul "and he fell to the ground" (Acts. 9. 4–9). And John writes: "When I saw him, I fell at his feet as though dead" (Rev. 1. 17).

Man is overwhelmed by the beauty of the Absolute when he

20. In this connection, look at a conversation from that curiously penetrating novel of Evelyn Waugh, *Brideshead Revisited*: "Often, almost daily, since I had known Sebastian, some chance word in his conversation had reminded me that he was a Catholic, but I took it as a foible . . . We never discussed the matter until on the second Sunday at Brideshead, when—we sat in the Colonnade . . . he surprised me by saying: 'Oh dear, it's very difficult being a Catholic.' 'Does it make much difference to you?' 'Of course. All the time.' 'Well, I can't say I've noticed it. Are you struggling against temptation? You don't seem much more virtuous than me.' 'I'm very, very much wickeder,' said Sebastian indignantly. 'Well then? . . . I suppose they try and make you believe an awful lot of nonsense?' 'Is it nonsense? I wish it were. It sometimes sounds terribly sensible to me.' 'But my dear Sebastian, you can't seriously *believe* it all.' 'Can't I?' 'I mean about Christmas and the star and the three kings and the ox and the ass.' 'Oh yes, I believe that. It's a lovely idea.' 'But you can't *believe* things because they're a lovely idea.' 'But I *do*. That's how I believe.' (*Brideshead Revisited*; London, 1960 edition, pp. 98–9).

experiences those heightened moments of life to which we have already referred. To show this is the present writer's intention. Human existence is seen as something experienced in and through God in whom man knows himself to have his final cause.[21] Human efforts to describe this we have called the referring back of human life to its ultimate cause.

Christian Anthropology

In Christ God became present to us. "That which was from the beginning, which we have heard, which we have seen with our eyes, which we have looked upon and touched with our hands . . ." (1 John 1. 1)—this refers to the Christ who "reflects the glory of God" (Hebr. 1. 3) in the world. For it is God "who has shone in our hearts to give the light of the knowledge of the glory of God in the face of Christ" (2 Cor. 4. 6). Christ became "once for all" (cf Hebr. 7. 27; 9. 11; 10. 10) the foundation of our belief. The Word of God "became flesh and dwelt among us" (John 1. 14). His power is gentle and still. In Christ we can "with unveiled face" behold "the glory of the Lord". We are even "being changed into his likeness" (2 Cor. 3. 18). "All things were created through him and for him. He is before all things, and in him all things hold together" (Col. 1. 15–20). As final point of convergence of all being[22] he transforms the world into

21. I should like to refer here to Hans Urs von Balthasar's still incomplete *Herrlichkeit. Eine theologische Ästhetik* (Einsiedeln, start of publication 1961), which has been called the most considerable Catholic work of the twentieth century in its field. For the first time beauty was deliberately placed at the centre of Catholic thought. For the first time, too, it was shown in such great detail that the revelation of God was made manifest in an "overwhelming of the spirit", gave proof of itself and showed itself in an illumination of being, in glory. In this way the beauty of Christ (*charis*) became the source of Christian life, thought and act. See too my article, Unerfreuliches und Ermutigendes (*Orientierung*, vol. 33, no. 22, November 30th 1969, pp. 244 ff).

22. All humanity and the whole world are contained in this illumination of being by God. See John 1. 29; 3. 16 f; 8. 12; 1 John 2. 2. The classic text is 1 Tim. 2. 1–6; Cf. Mt. 26. 28 and parallel texts; Mark 10. 45; Rom. 11. 32.

a dwelling place of glory, into a heavenly kingdom whose light is himself (Rev. 21. 23). The figure of the God-man, crowned in glory, is the depth, the goal and the fulfilment of human life.

And now we are in a position to explain the word Anthropology, mentioned above.

By *anthropology* we have in mind not so much a theory as an activity. Man sees himself as in the world, possessing the totality of meaningful life derived from the heightened moments of his experience. Through his life in the world, whose meaning he looks for in images invented by himself, he begins to understand himself as a being orientated towards the infinite. He understands his own infinity as limitlessly self-transcending, as the pull towards the eternal which is beyond the reach of his own efforts. For him, however, the unreachable is also a nearness that overwhelms him with the evidence of its presence, and brings him peace with its beauty, which is ultimately the primordial beauty of the Word become man—the loveliness and love for men of Christ. To follow this process with understanding[23] and to explain human life from this point of view is what we call "Christian Anthropology".

The attempt to understand man in depth, as sketched out here, can only be very fragmentary. At best it is an attempt to arrive at some kind of understanding of the mystery that is contained in the words spoken by Christ—"that they may have my joy fulfilled in themselves" (John 17. 13).

23. The word "understand" is usually employed in modern German philosophy in contradistinction (at least in the sense introduced by Dilthey) to "explain". Explanation is the method proper to the sciences. These look for "reasons", they refer things and events back to their effective causes, constituent elements and general laws, which determine them unambiguously. These methods are not suitable for the spiritual life and its objective manifestations. In the philosophy of religion the method of clarification was employed by, for example, Brunschwigg and Alain. The word "understand" as used in the religious sciences goes beyond "explanation" in trying to see the spiritual life as a development in meaning and value.

2. Threatened Man

WE now turn without delay to the problem of man threatened or endangered, for from it we intend to press forward into the realm of transcendence, which is seen by many as "a window into emptiness".[1] Human thinking goes to the heart of all human problems when it considers the nature of "threat" or "danger". The experience of being threatened or facing danger is the most universal and far-reaching experience of life. It is given far too little thought.[2] Danger is common to all human experience—that of every day and also the highest.

The biblical thinker, Jesus Sirach, gives us an astonishingly accurate description of human life:

> Much labour was created for every man,
>   and a heavy yoke is upon the sons of Adam,
> from the day they come forth from their mother's womb
>   till the day they return to the mother of all.
> Their perplexities and fear of heart –
>   Their anxious thought in the day of death,
> from the man who sits on a splendid throne
>   to the one who is humbled in dust and ashes,
> from the man who wears purple and a crown
>   to the one who is clothed in burlap;
> there is anger and envy and trouble and unrest,
>   and fear of death, and fury and strife.

1. This expression originates from the poet E. Burkart.
2. How often in recent times poets have filled the gap left by theologians—Bloy, Bernanos and Claudel—in France; Gertrud von Le Fort, and many who are concerned with Carmelite spirituality—in Germany.

And when one rests upon his bed,
  his sleep at night confuses his mind.
He gets little or no rest,
  and afterward in his sleep, as
    though he were on watch,
he is troubled by the vision of his mind
  like one who has escaped from the battle-front.

(Sir. 40. 1–6)

How painful is the path leading man to the state of high-minded resignation described by Paul: "We are afflicted in every way, but not crushed; perplexed, but not driven to despair; persecuted, but not forsaken; struck down, but not destroyed . . . I will all the more gladly boast of my weaknesses . . . I am content with weaknesses, insults, hardships, persecution, and calamities; for when I am weak, then I am strong" (2 Cor. 4. 8–9; 12. 9–10).

In the next few paragraphs we shall be considering the true meaning of life, thus obtaining the peace that comes from inner happiness. We shall try to break through the existing dangers and open our life to the bright light of day. For that is the meaning of miracles—a ready will to break out of the normal condition of things, and lift life out of itself. Miracles in their real sense are the most cherished possessions of religious life—to the great regret of many theologians and philosophers. Marvels and wonders in religion are the precise opposites of superstition. In them human awareness asserts itself against nothingness. The truth of miracles is this—that breaking asunder, breaking through, is possible. Miracles burst through the pre-salvation order of things. Something happens which, as Hegel described it, is an interruption, a "lightning flash, which all at once creates the order of a new world".[3] From out of the ordinary there are leaps into the extraordinary. The human will is impelled to believe in miracles not only through fear, need and uncertainty, but through attraction towards the light of a new world. Our experience

3. G. W. F. Hegel, *Phenomenology of Mind* (Introduction).

is not yet able to tell us of the new and unexpected manifestations that may appear in our life. Despite every kind of danger, there is in our difficult world a powerful urge towards salvation—an urge that can break through quite unexpectedly. The belief in miracles, if we consider its real meaning, is evidence of something pure, and not at all superstitious or fanatical, something which enables us to understand the real nature of our inner attraction towards the Absolute. Despite superficial appearances, there *is* a way from darkness to light.[4]

It would not of course be true to say that the experience of danger was basic to human life. There is something in life that the Bible calls "the love you had at first" (Rev. 2. 4). This is man's original love for the world, for the moments when he becomes aware of the existence of a mighty Being above him, when the divine breath bursts asunder all human limitations and carries him forward into the realm of the colourful and beautiful; man's first love when everything was still bathed in light and glowingly illumined; when he called things by their name and told them they were beautiful and good. Once man had a passionate love for the things of the world. He saw with astonishment what depths lay hidden in himself and what heights he could aspire to. Each discovery remained a pearl. Dreams went on their invisible way. The most beautiful dreams were of friendship and love. Other men's sufferings still had the power of distressing him intensely. He was still filled with a quiet reverence which made him fold his hands like the hands of children. All feeling of sufficiency was destroyed in him by a storm of longing. He was still able to cry for homesickness and struggle creatively in honest freedom. The clear flow of events brought gaiety into his soul. The world was still a place of superabundance. He could still marvel at women— the gentleness of their love, the delicacy of their feelings, their maternal protectiveness. He could still marvel at man—his protective power, his calm firmness, his sure guidance and clear knowledge.

4. For this explanation of "marvels" see also Ernst Bloch, *Das Prinzip Hoffnung* (Frankfurt a.M., 1959, vol. 2, pp. 1399 ff).

He was still able to laugh happily with those who were laughing—
but he could also cry with those who were weeping. Then, all of a
sudden, man's loving heart had turned to ashes. The misery of
human life was laid bare. Disgust filled his soul to its depths. He
stood there shuddering, with empty hands. Suddenly nothing new
was able to flower. The time had come of which the wise man in the
Bible spoke:

... Before the evil days come, and the years draw nigh, when you will
say, "I have no pleasure in them"; before the sun and the light and the
moon and the stars are darkened and the clouds return after the rain; in
the day when the keepers of the house tremble, and the strong men are
bent, and the grinders cease because they are few, and those that look
through the windows are dimmed, and the doors on the street are shut,
when the sound of the grinding is low, and one rises up at the voice of a
bird, and all the daughters of song are brought low, they are afraid also
of what is high, and terrors are in the way."

(Ecclesiastes 12. 1–5)

In this suddenly changed situation (which can give us the clearest
insights into life), we are made aware of the sadness of human existence. We experience what we earlier called "the common human
experience", "the salvation order of things" and "our difficult
world".[5] What is the meaning of man's subjection to suffering?
What is it in his life that makes it possible? John summarizes the
essence of human suffering in three heavily symbolic reports from
the pool of Bethzatha—the stories of the blind man, the lame and
the paralysed (John 5. 2–3). We shall discuss these three stories for
the light they shed on the condition of human life.

5. In his book on Kierkegaard, Romano Guardini has tried to mark out the
range and to make clear the inner dimension in which sadness, perhaps the
most painful phenomenon of life, has its being. See *Vom Sinn der Schwermut*
(Zürich, 1949, pp. 7–24).

The Blind Man

John shows us in what sense blindness is the description of our life
—"He who loves his brother abides in the light" (1 John 2. 10). Only
love opens our eyes and enables us to understand the meaning of
life.[6] Thus blindness quite simply means the inability to love.

What happens when, at break of day, darkness turns into light?
Things "appear". They break out of the silence of darkness, into
the world of appearances. They reveal themselves from within, open
up the essence of themselves, become distinct, individual, step out of
their enclosed world. Light reveals and creates the possibility of
self-revelation. Thus it is also the symbol of love. "Light did not
crush or do violence to what was revealed in the power of its
awakening call, but has freed it, has given it its own being from out
of the hiddenness of night, not banishing it into the unknown.
Light enters without reservation into the other, and yet withdraws
before the other." [7]

It keeps in the background, yet rouses to life. It is powerful only
when it does not obtrude, letting the other appear in all its variety.
Thus we can speak of the "purity" of light, of its beauty and self-
revelation. There is a depth of giving in light—and also in friendship and love—which, letting go of its own life, brings men and
things to life.[8] Love is a movement that sweeps clean. It is based on
the phrase "Volo ut sis"—I want you to be; and even more profoundly—I want you to *become more*. Love calls the other out of
itself into a mightier life. Love gives hope by opening up the future
for the loved one, and enabling him to become what he already was

6. See P. Rousselot, *Die Augen des Glaubens* (Einsiedeln, 1963), especially
the section entitled "Sicht durch Liebe", pp. 46–9; and R. Guardini, *Johanneische Botschaft* (Freiburg im Breisgau, 1962, no. 244, pp. 104 ff).

7. F. Ulrich, *Atheismus und Menschwerdung* (Einsiedeln, 1966, p. 26).

8. For an analysis of friendship and love see my *Der anwesende Gott. Wege
zu einer existentiellen Bewegung* (Olten, 1969, pp. 15 ff); *Meeting God in Man*
and *Mysterium Mortis*.

but had not yet become. Thus "volo ut sis" means—I want you to
fulfil your own life . . . I want you to become truly yourself at the
point where I myself become you . . . I want you to broaden out, to
extend yourself and open yourself out to the whole of reality . . . at
the precise point where I take my dwelling in you and merge totally
with you.[9]

Thoughts like these about "love as light" enable us to understand
the meaning of *lack of light*, for which we used the image of actual
blindness. Blindness is the attitude of groping towards, of taking
possession of. It does not let the other appear, and refuses him the
opportunity to expand. In its desire to be solely in charge, it un-
creates creation, and darkens life in the world. Thus it no longer has
anything in which it can lose itself and once more find itself. Its
own countenance gradually begins to darken, as it turns towards
darkness.[10]

If the basic formula of life illumined is "Self-becoming through
self-giving", then life become blind is "Self-destruction through
Self-assertion". This was the darkness into which Christ wanted to
send the rays of his glowing self. But the moment man no longer
experiences the brightness and sensitivity of heart that Augustine
called "lumen cordis",[11] friendship ceases and darkness gathers.
When this happens, man's indifference need not even take on terrible form. The darkness, in which the image of the other disappears,
began earlier, in hurtful words, in contemptuous thoughts, in poisonous feelings, in a judgment that condemns the fault of the other
without helping him to overcome it. When man lets all this emerge
within himself, the concept of human brotherhood grows weak in
him. Even the clearest words turn ambiguous, he sees intentions

9. F. Ulrich, *Atheismus und Menschwerdung* (Einsiedeln, 1966, p. 14).

10. Thomas Aquinas, "Esse ad lucem pertinet", in *Lib. de Causis*, 1, 6.

11. See Aurelius Augustinus Ep. 140, 22; 54 (Pl 33, 561; "Cordium lux
Deus") and Ep. 140, 25; 62 (Pl. 33, 565: "Vita cordium Christus"). Probably
the beautiful invocation of the Holy Spirit in the Church, "Veni lumen
cordium", comes from here (and also from John).

where there are none. He no longer walks with his brother in the light, but in darkness. Whether anything terrible happens then or not is entirely fortuitous. But which one of us can so master his own weariness that he constantly radiates a light which lights up other men and the world, and give them back their uniqueness? Which one of us possesses this "light of the heart"? We are more usually in a state of melancholy. Everything within us is heavy and dull. We do not possess a glowing heart but are possessed by the inner blindness of the small of soul who are unable to overcome their endless indifference, hostility and cruelty.[12]

The Lame Man

Then all of a sudden man—and in particular the good man—is seized by a weariness of heart. A feeling of inner lameness comes upon him and enters his soul. Where is that over-flowing life, that fountain from which sprang so much tenderness? Man becomes hard, shrivels up till he is nothing but exhaustion. A skeleton is all that remains, going about its tasks, without flesh or heart. He continues to be "good" out of habit, but it is a weary goodness, a painful goodness, full of an angry patience. Man now is "dried up" and can no longer be a source of anything to anyone. During such times he wishes he had no soul, but could live like the animals or vegetables; like animals that tremble or sing; or plants that need nothing save air, water and sun; like a dog that follows his master, unbothered by damnation or salvation. Man has the feeling that he is living at the very edge of the world. He could sleep day and night, letting himself slide into a miserable loneliness. Hope seems to be no longer there—the very hope that he once had nourished with the sweat of his brow.

Love, too, seems to be no longer available to him. A painful reality has broken him, body and soul. He asks himself: Will I always

12. See Guardini, *Johanneische Botschaft* (Freiburg im Breisgau, 1962), no. 244. See especially the section "Licht der Liebe", pp. 102 ff).

31

be one of those who demand nothing, who do not defend themselves, who let everything be taken away from them? Then insight comes: In my self-giving I followed—perhaps without knowing it—one who was condemned to death. Then the great temptation: I am weak; I can love neither God nor man; I can no longer see clearly; my heart has grown cold; virtue in me is at the end of its strength. Faith itself grows weak; there is no longer a trace of hope, on earth or in heaven. And within me there is the great uncertainty. If I do evil, I am never sure that it is evil; if I do good, I am never sure that it is good. If I say "Yes", I am not sure whether it is true. My soul moves restlessly between true and false, between good and evil.

As a child one was afraid when one bent over deep fountains, when one walked under the seemingly measureless height of cathedrals. But in those days there was someone there, a hand that took one's own, a voice that tempered the dizzy heights and depths. Now one is small again, but there is no hand any more; indeed, one has to give one's own hand to others. One increasingly becomes the victim of a curious disorder in things—things within and things without—which one can no longer set right. And always there is unquiet pain, the consequence of evil. One has given up studying it. What would be the use of that? One is afraid of the books that speak of it. They torture more than they bring relief. Who has an answer to all this? No one!

The good person and his despair—he has so greatly sighed with the suffering, he was so very dead with the dead, he took their anguish so much upon himself, and their despairing last breath, the increasing coldness of their limbs, that he suffers perhaps less from his own dissolution than from that which he endured on account of others. He knew God in his brother too deeply and too long, like Christ, who also threw himself to the ground in the hour of the "powers of darkness". This feeling of no longer being able to go on, this ceaseless surrender, was perhaps his (and our) final act of piety.[13]

13. It is perhaps appropriate at this point to refer to two books on the needs of Christian faith: R. Schneider, *Winter in Wien* (Freiburg im Breisgau, 1958) and M. Noël, *Erfahrungen mit Gott* (Mainz, 1961); a selection from the *Notes*

The Paralysed Man

It is precisely in his loss of the inner powers of life that man turns back to his original direction. Words may become empty, sure relationships waver, mystery becomes all-powerful, the sense of our own helplessness oppresses us. All this only shows that reality is to be looked for elsewhere. Dumbly man raises his empty hands towards God—perhaps not even with the feeling of longing, but in un-knowing self-giving.

Not even longing is what counts here, but something deeper and more fundamental which can only with difficulty be put into words: the longing for longing (*desiderium desiderii*), in which Ignatius of Loyola, with the intuition he brought to fundamentals, saw the deepest depths of human life.[14] There, in the depths of life reduced to its ultimate meaning, man begins to understand—This one thing cannot be taken away from me: not by my guilt or my weariness, not by my lack of faith or my darkness. Here man, perhaps weeping with pain and torment, remains secure and inviolable. It is this very experience of misery that shows him his own indestructibility and freedom from danger. Not even I myself, not even the darkest despair, can extinguish my deepest longing—"If only things were

---

intimes. I published a commentary on these two books a few years ago; "Reinhold Schneider und Marie Noël, Verzweiflung und Gnade unserer Zeit" (*Dokumente*, vol. 18, no. 5, October 1962, pp. 369 ff).

14. The relevant texts are to be found in *Primum ac Generale examen iis omnibus qui in Societatem Jesu admitti petent proponendum*. There (Caput IV, 45), Ignatius of Loyola says: "Quod si quis propter humanam nostram debilitatem ac miseriam, in se huiusmodi tam inflammata in Domino desideria non sentiret, interrogetur, an certe desiderium in se sentiat, huiusmodi desideria sentiendi." The first compiler of the Constitutions, H. Nadal, who was entrusted with this task by Ignatius himself, wrote at this point in his *Scholia in Constitutiones et Declarationes S.P. Ignatii*: "Si vero (quod fieri potest) negaverit se etiam desiderium illud desiderandi habere, eo omni studio ducendus est, nec recipiendus donec hac ex parte satisfaciat."

different!" There is a grace of human sorrows, the *"donum lacrimar-um"*. What happens now is the "weeping of the creature" that can go on no longer, but cannot stop wishing that it could go on. This is perhaps the most powerful urge towards human indestructibility, simply because it seems to happen against our own will. I cannot buy my own destruction, even at the price of despair. This is where I experience the meaning of true life, and am inevitably directed towards it.[15] This is the one thing that infinitely transcends me—the longing for longing.

None of this, of course, is subject to ordinary proof, because it acts directly on man's innermost being and does not allow any other perhaps more self-evident factor to intervene on its behalf. Here philosophy is truly summoned to the service of that which is revealed. But one of the most basic functions of religion is to put flesh upon human experiences by means of living images, so that those fleeting moments of true life will encompass the whole of life at the point where powers of imagination, insight, will, longing, feeling and vision all come together. The juxtaposition of concrete experiences with life as a whole leads to that dynamic movement which enables man to understand his own destiny.

Such images are powerful symbols of the archetypal events in our life, landmarks on the path of our own development. The symbol is a human figure bathed in blood, revealing the mystery of eternal life. We are not concerned for the moment with the actual historical events and happenings that lie at the back of this image raised to the measure, the constellation, of life.[16] This question belongs to the

15. Here I use an idea of M. Blondel's, which he expounded most fully in his *L'Action* (1893). *Essai critique de la vie et d'une Science de la Pratique* (new edition, Paris, 1950). Important for an understanding of Blondel's work is H. Bouillard's *Blondel et le christianisme* (Paris, 1961).

16. In this connection see these lines from R. M. Rilke's *Duino Elegies* (fourth Elegy, lines 76–8): "Who'll show a child just as it is? Who'll place it within its constellation, with the measure of distance in its hand?" R. Guardini says of this: "The figure of the child grows into the immeasurable: 'Just as it is?'—Who can show this? To place a human life 'within its con-

sphere of "history", a decision founded on the exploration of the past—whereas our exposition is directed towards the present experience of life. This is not to cast doubt on the historicity of the events which go to form the shape of destiny. It is only that it is irrelevant to the purpose of classifying life, and is thus ruled out for us in advance.

Man endangered, and yet eternally free from danger, can best be understood from the symbolic story of the prophet Elijah. We shall briefly describe it here, as it is recorded in the Elijah chapters 17 to 22 of the First Book of Kings, and the Elisha chapters 1 and 2 of the Second Book of Kings.

The life and destiny of the prophet Elijah are summarized in their essentials in the Wisdom literature. Jesus Sirach describes him as follows:

> Then the prophet Elijah arose like a fire,
>   and his word burned like a torch.
> He brought a famine upon them,
>   and by his zeal he made them few in number.
> By the word of the Lord he shut up the heavens,
>   and also three times brought down fire.
> How glorious you were, O Elijah, in your wondrous deeds!
>   And who has the right to boast which you have?
> You have raised a corpse from death
>   and from Hades, by the word of the Most High;

---

stellation' derives from the myths. What is meant by the word 'who' is not a human being but a power; the power that, in the myths, lifts up extraordinary men, those who have lived their human life heroically, to the stars; away from the earth to the heavens; out of the temporal to the eternal; away from the changing to the permanent . . . And (this constellation of the child) should have the 'measure of distance' in its hand. This measure determines the difference between it and the world, where intelligence, purpose and agreement are to be found." Rainer Maria Rilke's *Deutung des Daseins* (Munich, 1953, pp. 178 f, translated by J. B. Leishman and Stephen Spender, London, 1939; revised edition, 1948).

who brought kings down to destruction,
    and famous men from their beds;
who heard rebuke at Sinai
    and judgments of vengeance at Horeb;
who anointed kings to inflict retribution,
    and prophets to succeed you,
You who were taken up by a whirlwind of fire,
    in a chariot with horses of fire;
you who are ready at the appointed time, it is written,
    to calm the wrath of God before it breaks out in fury,
to turn the heart of the father to the son,
    and to restore the tribes of Jacob.
Blessed are those who saw you,
    and those who have been adorned in love;
    for we also shall surely live.

(Sir. 48. 1–11)

The letter of James in the New Testament asserts that we can recognize ourselves in him: "Elijah was a man of like nature with ourselves" (James 5. 17).

He suddenly appears out of the silent unknown. A man of fire enters the wild confusion of time. We do not discover where he acquired his power, how he has become as he is. We learn only one thing—that he was filled with immense life and let himself be consumed by zeal. Again and again he uttered the cry, "The Lord God lives". He threw himself into the battle against the mighty ones, who lived in hardened pride in the glory of their victories and their success, and oppressed the little ones and the defenceless. But he waged his real battle against that "nothingness', in which the prophets have always recognized the essence of idolatory. Idols are pure appearances, empty externals, behind whom there is only a void. Elijah fought against this nothingness with acts and words that came down like lightning.

When the spirit came upon him, he was able to run, talk, speak words of power, offer resistance to the last breath, threaten and place himself on the side of the oppressed. It is true that there were

36

quiet times also in his life—for example the quiet time of retirement by the brook Cherith. The ravens brought him bread and meat in the morning and the evening, and he drank from the clear water of the brook. He met with the delicate gentleness of a broken woman whose dearest possession in life he returned to her. But this holy life in him was in constant peril. Fear fell upon him, the spirit was suddenly no longer present, he was given over to external loneliness. The stream of his life had dried up. Thereupon he fled from the threatening emptiness, away from men's nearness, into the desert of loneliness, the wilderness of life. Not even his servant could follow him in his flight. All excellence suddenly left him. He had burnt himself out, inwardly and outwardly.

Now he desired death, perhaps he even sought death out, as he strode with his last strength into the deserted wasteland. Thus he falls into the deep sleep of oblivion, wakens and then falls asleep again under the scanty shade of a sparse bush in the desert. And it becomes clear to him that the flight from danger was a longing for life, for stillness, for the absolute. This ultimate longing (personified in the figure of the angel)[17] raises him up again and again and lets him go on to the mountain Horeb, to God. He finds shelter in a cave on the holy mountain.

In the darkness between the rocks he now proceeds to question his soul: What are you seeking, you sole survivor among the prophets? What are you looking for in life? Elijah has thrown himself with burning zeal into work for the living God, and in so doing has become a fugitive who has separated himself from the world. Suddenly he notices a curious thing. The mountain was trembling under

17. We note here the angelic appearances around the prophet Daniel who was called by the angel "greatly beloved" (Dan. 9. 23). It was the angel Gabriel, whose name is interpreted variously as "strong man of God", "God has shown himself strong" and "he who stands before God". It is the first time that an angel in the Bible is given a name. (See Dan. 8. 16–26; 9. 21–27.) See too Luke 1. 19. Perhaps these references may enable us to call angels "points of mediation and concretization of human longing".

a mighty storm, rocks rolled down it. That was my life, but it was not God. Lightning strikes, the mountain glows in the brightness. That was my life, but it was not God. Everything trembles under the force of the storm. This trembling was my life, but it was not God. And then, all of a sudden, everything is over, as happens when mountain storms suddenly cease. The clouds lighten, the wind slows down. Elijah steps out of the darkness of the cave and hears the quiet rustle of a breath of wind, and feels it on his face. Then it happens—This was the longing of my heart from the beginning. It was what I was from the beginning, but have never become: stillness, rest, gentle touch, unobtrusive being. Thereupon Elijah wraps his face in his mantle, for the mystery is so near him now that he can only stand before it in blind surrender.

Now he understands that there is nothing left to him save stillness, save the silent encounter. In order to keep the people on the path they should go, he comes down from the mountain to look for someone to continue his prophetic destiny.[18] He finds Elisha who follows him and does not want to let him be, until he slowly learns to understand the mystery of silence. Restlessly the two men wander from place to place. People are taken aback, they have a presentiment of the mystery of his stillness and withdrawal. Elijah had hidden his face before the felt presence of God—he did not dare the ultimate. He was not strong enough to look God in the face. Finally the thought comes to him—one must, one should, one could, face that last vision of all. The highest cannot be death for men. Man must be able to endure it, even in his present state.[19] Elisha tells all the friends of Elijah that they must be still. When the final moments of a

18. O. Schneider puts the events related in the 21st chapter of the First Book of Kings before the seventeenth chapter (see *Elias*, Schöning, Paderborn, 1962, p. 17), in view of J. Steinmann's research. But I see the existing order as more authoritative in settling this important question.

19. This "being able to endure" God (the demand of the "unveiled face of God") is the basis and the real meaning of the Catholic teaching of "Purgatory". Before God man can only stand "with upright courage" (Ernst Bloch). See my exposition in *Mysterium Mortis* (Walter, Olten, 1968, pp. 138 ff).

life are coming to an end, they must be met in silence, surrounded by human stillness. Thus they wander silently into the wilderness. Suddenly they are separated by another appearance of fire, and Elijah is carried away in a chariot of fire drawn by glowing horses into eternal life. Only his prophet's mantle remained lying on the sand of the wilderness.[20] With the same suddenness with which he came out of the unknown and appeared in the world of men, he disappeared again amidst signs and wonders.

We must not spoil this story of a life, its uniqueness and compactness, its symbolism, by further interpretations. The story as it has been told here is already sufficiently explained.[21] We are now—in the light of our phenomenological intention—ready to some extent to explore the archetypal situation which we have prepared for here. Man is threatened, not only by external powers and events, but still more by the very fact of his manhood. In this situation, where threats come from all sides, he is brought back to the essence of his situation. And thereby his own indestructibility is made known to him. The more man moves forward into the mystery, the more peaceful his life becomes. No limits can be set to his growth in contentment, since the gift he is given is inexhaustible. Thus human life consists of longing, forever increasing and forever fulfilled.

All these painfully collected fragments of ideas must now be seen in their totality, if we want to get a glimmer of understanding about the fundamental reality concerning man—the reality to which human language has given the name "immortality" as an indication of the goal towards which it is moving. Faced by threats on all sides, man comes increasingly to understand about grace in life, his own life, which from the beginning is eternal life with body and soul.

20. See P. Teilhard de Chardin, *Hymne de l'Univers*, Paris, 1961, pp. 71–75; Eng. trans. *Hymn of the Universe*).

21. This interpretation was primarily based on the order of events related, the stressing of the most important elements, and the omission of unimportant details; and also on the emphasis in the story telling of the inner meaning. That this is a justifiable exegetical method is shown by H. de Lubac.

Now comes the first definition of human existence in the anthropology we are endeavouring to work out here:—Man is the being who, despite dangers all around him, can experience the reality of an absolute other.

And finally we should like to add two further clarifications which bring the lines of our argument to their final conclusion.

First: It seems to us that this absolute other, whose presence we discovered in the experiences recounted above, cannot simply be called "God". The direction of human life developing under the burden of threats tends towards something more—perhaps only unconsciously and unthematically, but nevertheless in reality. Threatened man, in order to be eternally safe, needs more than a "God" whom he cannot look upon with lifted face, a "God" who is himself only a further threat to him. It is now that man, worn down by his sufferings, departs from his beautifully complete concept of God and looks for a Being to protect him from his God's threats. Like Job, who in a final upsurge of hope, rears up against all threats:

> Why do you, like God, pursue me?
>   Why are you not satisfied with my flesh?
> . . .
> For I know that my Redeemer lives,
>   and at last he will stand upon the earth;
> and after my skin has been thus destroyed,
>   then from my flesh I shall see God,
> Whom I shall see on my side,
>   and my eyes shall behold, and not another.
> My heart faints within me!
>
> (Job 19. 22–27)

Out of a surface wrangling with God there grows an image of a man-like God, one who, indeed, becomes man. Under the enormous pressures of suffering, out of the experience of danger on all sides, there comes a God who is also encompassed by danger, a God who gives his life for his friends, who, as Word that has become flesh, is able to undergo the experience of death, who opens up for us another depth and another height than those in which man up to then has seen his God—"the love of God in Christ Jesus Our Lord" (Rom. 8. 39). Man longs for a God who is like men, his brothers, in all things, so that he might become "merciful" (Hebr. 2.17); a God who is "beset with weakness", who "can deal greatly with the ignorant and wayward", because "in every respect [he] has been tempted as we are, yet without sinning"; who "offered up prayers and supplications, with loud cries and tears", who was "heard for his godly fear" (see Hebr. 5. 2; 4. 15; 5. 7). The ultimate depths of God-awareness take on flesh here, in the God-man, who is the object of all the longings directed towards the Absolute. "He who has seen me has seen the Father" (John 14. 9)—the Father who no longer calls us "servants" but "friends" (John 15. 15). This movement towards Christ, like every grace in our order of salvation, must be called the grace of Christ.

Second: The man who evades the threats directed against himself —which for the greater part consist in bearing his brother's sufferings, closes his own way to that immeasurable joy that can break out in the cry of jubilation: "We have found the Messiah!" (John 1. 41) And this is true also the other way round. Every act of endurance, of bearing to the end and in silence the human situation of danger, can become a starting point for the break-through to the God of our life.

3. Silent Man

SILENCE is a fundamental fact of life. It opens up the finite world to the infinite. In this chapter we shall ask ourselves about the nature of being, and what causes it to behave as it does, finding in the experience of silence the clearest revelation of the Absolute.[1] There exists, of course, also a "negative silence", a dumb rebelliousness, an unfathomable hostility, a dull lack of interest. We shall ignore these gloomy aspects of human silence and turn to that positive silence which the experience of a personal interior life can call into being.

Always, but above all in our present age of many words and discoveries, silence counted as one of the most noble virtues. In a talkative world,[2] man loses the ability of direct experience. We see this most clearly in an extraordinary activity engaged in by people of not inconsiderable intelligence—the activity we call "discussion" or "analysis", taking to pieces. In conversation ideas are set out in such a way that everyone can follow them equally. But this is only possible when the conversation (and therefore also our whole life) acquires a level of sameness. As we continue to talk, our words are separated from ourselves and become common currency. Finally we can no longer distinguish between really creative thinking and what was simply said in imitation. Thus human life loses its roots and becomes disorientated. In such a situation silence must be learnt anew. We must return to our own actual

1. See in my book (including the notes), *Der anwesende Gott* (Olten, 1969), the section entitled "Das Schweigen", pp. 197 ff.
2. See M. Heidegger, *Sein und Zeit* (Tübingen, 1953, pp. 167, 169, 170, 175; Eng. trans., *Being and Time*, London, 1967).

experience, to the mystery that cannot be talked about but must be adored.

If we want to understand the essence of silence, we need only think of those moments in life when the silence of love becomes a reality for us. We are referring to the delicate mutual understanding of those in love or of friends, which can perfectly express itself in mere being together, jointly contemplating. From this point there are gradations in the silence of love, leading up to a mystical silence together, as it has been recorded of the follower of St Francis, Egidius, and the saintly French King, Louis, who met each other on one occasion but said not a word, only—we are told—"saw each other reflected in the mirror of the divine countenance." [3] There is a four-fold meaning in all this.

3. "St Louis, king of France, who was on his way to join the seven-year old Crusade to the holy places, had been told of the high repute in which Brother Egidio was held, and decided to pay him a visit. He came to Perugia for this purpose and when he learnt that Brother Egidio was staying there, knocked on his door, clad like a poor pilgrim, with only a few companions, and begged to see him. The doorkeeper went to Brother Egidio and told him that a stranger had come to see him. But Brother Egidio immediately knew by the Holy Spirit who his visitor was. Drunk with joy he hastened to the door from his cell and there the two fell into each other's arms, greeting each other with a holy kiss. They fell down before each other as though they were old friends, and gave each other signs of devoted love. But neither of them said a word. They stayed like this in total silence till they bade each other farewell. When St Louis was departing, one of the Brothers asked one of his followers who it was who had so lovingly greeted Brother Egidio on his knees. "King Louis of France," was the answer. "He is on his way to the Crusade, and wanted to see the Holy brother Egidio." The Brothers, on hearing this, were indignant and said to Egidio, "How could you be so stupid and say nothing to so great a king who has come from France to see you and to hear you speak?" "My dear Brothers," he replied, "do not be astonished that neither he nor I had anything to say to one another. For as soon as we embraced, his heart was opened to me by the light of divine vision, and mine to him. And we saw everything in the mirror of eternity. What he had wanted to say to me, and what I had planned to say to him, we said much better in silence, without sound from lips or tongue, by way of direct consolation, than if we

First: We experience our own life as Openness, as readiness to remove all barriers, to receive the Other into ourselves in all his uniqueness and individuality. In such moments, silence is the mark of openness. We dare not speak of the experience of being together because we know that no words can express our happiness. Wordless understanding is a sign that we experience the Other as something holy and do not want to profane it even by words. We wish only that this Other remain and abide with us. We want nothing from it, only to do well by it, to be good to it. This is a further step in the "silence of love".

Second: The silence of love signifies an exchange of presence. When we are silent, we do not experience and receive "something", but "someone". One cannot reduce this to individual elements and qualities. Perhaps it might be possible to describe and analyse the characteristics of a beloved person. But this is not what makes up the reality of love, the uniqueness of the Other. That is why a loving relationship not only increases but transforms our relationship to the world. Something that cannot be exacted is given in a surrender before which one can only be silent. The beloved Other is not one of the numerous contents of the world that we can know and experience. It is the source of our experience of all other contents and statements, because it includes them all and opens itself up to them. The talk of love thus confines itself almost always to saying how the world has been changed by the experience of love's presence. The presence itself is mostly received in silence, and with it also the actual mystery of love. Here we already come to a new aspect of love's silence.

Third: The silence of love comes as an overwhelming experience. The person who loves cannot explain the mystery of the received

---

had spoken together by word of mouth. And if we had expressed in words what we inwardly felt, the words would have been disappointing, not joy-making. So now you can understand why he departs joyfully." (*Fioretti/ Blütenlegende*, extract from Francis of Assisi, *Legenden und Laude*. Ed. with commentary by O. Karrer, Zürich, 1945; pp. 431–3.)

Presence, cannot unveil its mystery by means of words. The person knows immediately that he has found something from which, in which and out of which he can live, if only he does not destroy the mystery of the Other as Presence. But the Other is ours only in its withdrawnness and intangibility. We have come to know the Other, but at the same time we have no "knowledge" of it which qualifies or diminishes its mystery. If this were to happen, then the Other would have become a thing, would cease to be the Other of our life. If one wanted to formulate the hardness of this paradox, one could express the experience of love as follows: We have received nothing in love, and by that very fact have gained everything. What one of the subtlest thinkers of Christendom, Nicholas von Kues, the teacher of the "knowing unknowingness" (*docta ignorantia*) has said of our relationship to God, is in essence true of every experience of friendship and love. One of his shortest writings, which bears the strange title "A conversation between two men, one of whom is a pagan, the other a Christian, about the hidden God" describes a dramatic situation. The pagan enters a church and sees a Christian in adoration. He is deeply moved by such devotion and speaks to the Christian. And now begins a conversation whose first sentence describes with astonishing conciseness the essence of what we have tried to say above: "The pagan: I see that you, bowing down, filled with reverence, from out of a full heart, are weeping tears of love, but without dissembling: Tell me please who you are! The Christian: I am a Christian. The Pagan: Whom do you worship? The Christian: God. The Pagan: Who is the God, whom you worship? The Christian: I do not know. The Pagan: How can you worship so seriously something that you do not know? The Christian: I worship Him precisely because I do not know him."[4]

Here the reality of a beloved Other is not put in doubt. On the

4. N. von Kues, *Ein Gespräch zweier Männer, von denen der eine Heide, der andere Christ is, über den verborgenen Gott* (Philosophisch-theologische Schriften, Vol. 1, Vienna, 1964, pp. 300 f).

contrary—man refuses to place his Presence in a row of other experiences. By contrast with all other knowledge, the Presence of the beloved must be seen as the unknown and the unfathomable.

Fourth: The man who has experienced the presence of love possesses an ultimate security. In being taken over by the beloved Other, he sees the whole world with new eyes. He cannot, it is true, answer the questions of life more easily. But somehow his life has become clearer. Every need and every experience was made less than real by the presence of the Other. Essentially nothing counts any longer. Man begins to understand, despite all anxieties, that ultimately everything is secure. This ultimate security has been given him in the beloved Other, and no one can any longer take it away from him.

Every real silence contains these four basic elements: Being opened up, the Presence, being overwhelmed by, and being given meaning. Thus one could describe human silence as follows—life opened up and overwhelmed by a meaningful Presence. If we now go on to examine human silence for its transcendental meaning, we have to delve further. In various experiences of silence human life makes discoveries which lead directly to the experienced presence of the Absolute. The first development, the aspect of silence best known and most available to us, is—

Hearing

As experience in life (and not merely as partial event), human hearing means that someone takes into himself what a stranger has to say about himself. But this presupposes a prior disposition, a basic ability, to receive the truth of another life; a living relationship therefore. What is remarkable here is that man feels an unlimited readiness in himself to comprehend the communication of being—that he feels himself related not only to men but to being as such. *"Nihil a me alienum puto"*—"I consider nothing alien to me". Terence's statement, changed and put into more radical form

(*Homo sum; humani nihil a me alienum puto*—I am man; I consider nothing human alien to me) is the archetypal condition of all hearing, an instinctive conviction, through hearing and making hearing possible, that all things are related to one another.

But we must explore still further. One of the finest achievements of human thought is the form of philosophy known by the collective name "transcendental philosophy", which tries to clarify this conviction from various points of view and by means of rich and sensitive reductions.[5] This philosophy has succeeded in throwing light on the origin, unknown to us and intuitively perceived, of the experience which we see as the individual perception of things (in our case the concrete, limited content of what we "hear").

In every concrete attempt at truth (or hearing) there enter all the voices of the world, there enters life itself. This "listening in" to the world is the necessary precondition for "hearing". The voice of the finite "other" is perceived against the background of the sounding, surging waves of the "All" which are continually rolling towards us, yet are not specifically perceived by us. In each individual voice we hear all the voices of the world. Life itself possesses a character of "word and voice", and communicates itself to us in advance. Individual hearing is thus only a "calling into the recollection" of something we have always known. It is not our task to expound here the philosophical details of this transcendental reduction, especially as we are of the opinion that they are only trying to express an archetypal experience of human life which, in the course of coming into being, approaches every man with overwhelming proof.

The seemingly meaningless words of love thus acquire a life-illuminating significance. A single act of personal love is sufficient to fill the entire horizon of the universe, from the lowest being to the highest. When one who loves says, "You are everything to

5. Here I merely refer readers to K. Rahner's "Hörer des Wortes" (Munich, 1963). Perhaps I should add that the "transcendental reduction" must be continued in the personal sphere.

me," or, the other way round, "Without you everything is meaningless," he is, all unknown to himself, not realizing the importance
of his words—uttering an entire metaphysics of man's anticipation
of the totality of being.[6] Whenever a listener's receptiveness becomes intense, it acquires a direction of its own. Then we speak
of—

Listening

It is the significance of the message that turns simple "hearing" into
"listening". Man forgets, if only for a moment, the importance of
his own life. He is simply present, intent on the Other. It is an
atmosphere in which he can understand life-giving words. Perhaps
only familiar ideas are communicated in this way. But they open
up their deepest meaning here. Almost every word seems new and
profoundly moving. This happens occasionally when the words
spoken break through the human ability to listen.

Thus man can experience, by careful listening, the "more" of the
world, of things, and of the Other. He understands that in every
created thing there is more than that thing needs to be as it is. The
world is not made according to a strict measure of sufficiency, but
with the fullness of being. "A flower, for example, does not send its
seed by the quickest route, as it were through a funnel, for the next
year's blooms, but flowers in an over-abundance of colours. These
colours have a value of their own, and the fall of the seeds is inci-
dental. The flower is present in its fullness, in the fullness of life,
and not because this is the easiest and quickest way for it to repro-
duce itself."[7]

6. This is where man can understand the invitation to open himself up to
the (perhaps still anonymous) Presence of an (as yet indefinite) Absolute,
where the free gift of grace can enter into him, the reception of a "more",
a "heartfelt expectation of the unknown Messiah" (Blondel).

7. M. Picard, *Das Mehr*, in the Przywara-Festschrift, *Der beständige
Aufbruch* (Nuremberg, 1959).

It is of course also true that one can fail to hear the words of the Other. A simple word is spoken by a normally withdrawn person who is usually incapable of communicating. And suppose that at this very moment the iron bands round our hearts are ready to fall. The speaker gathers all his forces together and speaks a word, unskilfully and unclearly perhaps, but still the "word" of his life. But the man who hears him does not understand, does not listen, whether out of tiredness or relaxation of tension, or again because the noise of his own self is louder than anything coming to him from outside. So the word is lost, falls on unfruitful ground, disappears in the emptiness. And thus life can fall back into a helpless inability to communicate oneself, into non-recognition.

But if there should come about an attitude of listening and attending, then the world begins to open up. The words perhaps become more sparse, but for this very reason they are more tightly packed. They take on an inward glow. The "more" of the world is lying open before us, delivered over to our love.[8] The attitude of listening leads almost imperceptibly to the state of a still more intense silence, the silence of—

Watching and Waiting

The person who has experienced the mutual relationship and the inner "more" of things in hearing and listening, is calm and hospitable towards all things. Watching and waiting is this very sense of hospitality towards everything that exists, the ability of love to hear still voices, to guess at unexpressed or only hinted at feelings, to be with the other in his hidden pain and secret need, to welcome shyly offered feelings of friendship, to be responsive to the least movement of the world. The smallest and most insignificant trifle then becomes a symbol of the mystery. The attentive man can even hear the voice of nature. Stones, flowers and trees all speak

8. See M. Buber, *Einsichten* (Wiesbaden, 1953, pp. 6–8; 26–7).

to him. He receives these voices silently into his own self. His life moves with them. The signs of the world, to which he has become attentive, turn into part of his own inner life, are no longer distinguishable from himself, and reveal to him the meaning of the world. He gently welcomes them in the attitude of watching and waiting, and by slow degrees they become part of him.

One can, for example, listen attentively to a spring of water gushing down a mountain. From the depths of the earth there emerges, under powerful pressure, this flowing gift. All of a sudden man perceives a correspondence in himself—This is myself, he thinks, this occurs again and again in my own life. One must look for the spring in one's life, and when one has found it, one must grasp hold of it, cleanse it, cherish it, or else it trickles away into the sand. Thus man recognizes the flow of his own life. The same is true, too, of a flame. It must be lit, then it will send out both light and warmth. It is small, trembling, flickering. And it feeds upon itself. But in an unguarded moment it can do terrible damage. Man understands the comparison at once—This is my own life, my thoughts, wishes, feelings, my understanding. Thus he begins to grasp, silently attentive, the life-explanatory mystery of the world— the mystery of the wave, of the way, of the tree, the garden, the house, the mystery of battle and of many other things in the world.[9] By means of such ideas the "other things", the "holy things" of the world, enter into his understanding. They are woven into his feelings and thoughts, his ideas, acts and dreams. They bring rest, drive away evil thoughts and preserve life from chaos.

Thus can man all of a sudden—and this is the essence of "watching and waiting"—perceive with moving clarity the symbolic nature of things. Everything in the world is a symbol, a likeness of the one, original and ungraspable thing, is fragment and articulation of a still greater Other. Life itself is the "spring" and the "flame". That is why, and to this extent alone, there can be spring and flame

9. R. Guardini, *Das Verblassen der Bilder* (from my notes of Guardini's lecture to the Bavarian Academy, 16th November 1953).

at all. In the experience of likeness, the whole of human life is trans-
formed. We do not come to know the Absolute through knowing
things, but from our experience of the Absolute we obtain the
power to grasp the finite. Our effort until now "to find God in all
things" thereby acquires a deeper meaning. Indeed it gets reversed
into "to find all things in God". It is not our experience of things
that points to God, but God who points, from the beginning and
in advance of all, to the world of things. It is not God who must be
found, but the world, in His likeness, that comes to life before our
God-filled eyes. The Absolute is the original Presence of the human
spirit, unnamed perhaps, unpronounced and unfulfilled, but no less
real. Its presence is a constant reminder—Here am I.

> I was ready to be sought by those
>   who did not ask for me;
> I was ready to be found by those
>   who did not seek me.
> I said, "Here am I, here am I.'
>
> (Is. 65. 1–2)

Out of this transformation of the world of our experience through
the experience of likeness, grows the attitude in which human
silence reaches its ultimate depth and to which we give the name—

Hearing and Obeying

In the experience of obeying we are taking hold of the finite in its
relation to the infinite and thus giving it a new centre of gravity.
The reality of the transcendental is set free in the world. Thus man
learns that he can himself be the "word of God" for others, as
others have become for him the "word of God". In his own threatened and perhaps also unfulfilled life, the presence of God in the
world will be made manifest. No man can feel ready for such a
destiny. Life as mission is a call upon our frailty. The letter to the
Romans formulates this "sending" in a terrifying paraphrase of
Deuteronomy (30. 11–14): "Do not say in your heart, 'Who will

ascend into heaven?' (that is, to bring Christ down), or 'Who will descend into the abyss?' (that is, to bring Christ up from the dead). But what does it say? The word is near you, on your lips and in your heart" (Rom. 10. 6–8).

In our own life Infinite Being turns towards the world! This knowledge tears down the thin layers of our self-confidence so that we are able to see at last how our inner life is constricted by lies, entangled in cunning, deception and hypocrisy: how our inner self, where our being is lost to us in darkness, is ruled by wickedness; how our entire being is made up of trivialities; fragments, divisions and chance encounters; how it is conditioned by fickle human situations and coloured by changing human moods. Can such a life become the word of God for the world? Now man begins to obey the voice of God, humbly to ask to speak to him. The image of God begins more and more to realize itself in him; the Absolute enters ever more deeply into the fabric of his life, till it becomes in truth a word of God, till God himself becomes present when he quietly holds out his hands to man. In such obedience the whole of life is involved. Only the infinite will be free of presuppositions, friendly and at peace. Where such selfless surrender is found, there God himself is present. Man becomes messenger, sign and witness of the Absolute.

Thus there unfolds before us the beautiful image of silent man, out of whose innermost life bursts God himself, even if unwilled and unsummoned. Thus silent man is all these—existence opened up, life in the present, destiny overcome, experience of ultimate meaning. And the perception of the relationship of all things, the experience of the "more" in the world, the grasp of the quality of likeness in all creation, become for us living signs of the presence of the Absolute. Such a life is still not "proof" of God, but it is an indication of God.[10] Man therefore is that being in whose silence the presence of God takes place for us.

10. See J. Moltmann, *Theologie der Hoffnung* (Munich, 1965, p. 53. See also note 61 on the same page; Eng. trans.: *Theology of Hope*, London, 1968).

This is our second attempt to define man's essence, but we shall go on further, in order to be able to grasp the totality of human life in all its richness.

The phenomenological method, which we are following in this investigation, has no other possibility of verification than so to un- cover the inner form of a truth or an event that it overwhelms the mind. As the inner form of truth of the statement "Silence is the place of encounter with God", the Bible tells the story of the pro- phet Samuel. He is a figure surrounded by legends—the figure of a wise, gentle and incorruptible man who serves truth, and whose divine power was invoked from out of the depths of the earth for an entire historical era after his death (Cf. Sir. 46, 13–20; see also 1 Sam. 10. 1; 16. 1–13 (the anointing of Saul and David); 1 Sam. 7. 10 (the miracle of the thunder); 1 Sam. 12. 1–7 (his way of life); 1 Sam. 28. 1–25 (the calling up of the dead). But all his inner strength lay concealed in the figure of a child. We are introduced to an entire metaphysic of childhood here.

Samuel's birth was the result of his mother's humiliation. She was barren, made sad by the hurtful words of her rival, and weighed down by sorrow. Her grieving soul was filled with longing for a child. She prayed for a child. This prayer of her deepest need was heard by God. She looked on the child she bore as the fruit of her worship and gave him the name Samuel—"I have asked him of the Lord." Within her the feeling grew that this small child did not belong to her but to God. With joyful heart she broke into the "Magnificat" of the Old Dispensation, Hannah's song of praise, and left the dearest thing in her life in the "House of the Lord at Shiloh", under the care of the aged, weak-willed, but in his fashion deeply God-committed priest, Eli.

The mother visits the boy once a year, and brings him a little linen robe in which he ministers before the Lord. The child's life is lonely. The sons of the aged Eli are rough and brutal companions. But old Eli is very fond of the child. It is not, however, people who make up the real environment of the Child but the presence of the Mystery, whose sign is the ark of God in the temple at Shiloh.

Sentences like "The boy Samuel grew in the presence of the Lord"; "The boy Samuel continued to grow both in stature and in favour with the Lord and with men" describe in their simplicity the closeness to God of a quiet and thoughtful child, who used to sleep before the Ark, in the "presence of God", as in the arms of God. The nights are still and silent. Only a small lamp burns before the Ark. Everything is pregnant with meaning, is filled with the presence of the Mighty One. And it all flows into the child's receptive soul. Knowledge of God grows in this seclusion. The world transcends itself in this small place. The child knows about God, as a child knows with its whole being the presence of its mother— knows it as the warm gentleness of life. Yet the text explicitly says: "Samuel did not yet know the Lord." This means that the presence of God, which is felt in silence, had not yet been brought to his consciousness.

But suddenly the silence turns into a cry, "Samuel! Samuel!" The child wakens, and speaks in the silence of the night, "Here I am!" He runs at once to the old man, Eli, wakes him from his sleep, and says to him, "You called me." The old man sends him back to sleep. The same thing happens three times, until the wise old man understands that here, in this tender child, something extraordinary was taking place—the coming of God into human life. He sends him back to sleep, with the instruction that Samuel, if called again, should reply, "Speak, Lord." Thus out of a silent hiddenness with God there emerges Samuel's destiny. All his life Samuel remained true to the words of the silent mystery: "Samuel grew, and the Lord was with him and let none of his words fall to the ground."

It only remains for us here to point out how, in the experience of stillness, there grows up in man an understanding of a God of warm human nearness, a God of goodness and compassion in whose unobtrusive manhood every need is met and fulfilled; a God-man whose nature is mildness and quiet simplicity, who is always present when man speaks to him in despair, misery and hopelessness; a God who in his goodness and stillness lets himself be used by men, giving peace to everyone—unceasing, eternal peace; a God who begs for our love, who knows enmity and fear, who can kneel before us in humility. Christ is no stranger to us. He is the essence of everything that is true, quiet and compassionate. Behind the veil of his humanity his true face is already visible. Silent man knows him for a brother, even if he has never heard of him.

Thus we come to understand the meaning of stillness for our human condition. Truly to become a figure of a still man in the world means to make God himself perceptible as the presence of Christ. Hearing, listening, attending, obeying is how this transformation takes place. In man's soul there will be much suffering and fearful despair. But again and again he will quietly open up his life to the Mystery, so that God-made-man can make of everything that is a new creation.

Never has our world needed so many still people as now. And perhaps there have never been so few. The man to whom is given today the experience of stillness must be grateful for it, cherish it, and see that it becomes fruitful. But if he knows nothing about it, he must at least begin with the serious tasks of every day.

4. Friendly Man

MAN can turn towards God as the result of various experiences. We ought not to list them according to precedence, for basically all human experience is experience of the transcendental, or could lead man to experience it. But it is surely permissible to put certain experiences more specially into the foreground, to refer to them with special reverence, because they are nearer to our heart than others. Thus in this chapter we want to examine human friendship for the mystery contained in it, but with the same delicacy that man usually brings to those personal parts of his life. When we speak of "man as friend", we do not simply mean that he is well-intentioned towards others, attentive, sympathetic, kind or indulgent. We are using the phrase in its original meaning, as an expression of man's very being—something that enables him to come close to the real self of another. We are not speaking here of the measurable and tangible but of encounters.

Where does such a man stand in life? From where does he obtain the strength to see other men not simply in the fact of their bodily presence, but in that special aspect where they are "themselves" and "brothers"? What kind of world opens out to such a man? What horizons of self-awareness reveal themselves to him?[1]

The Insecurity of Human Existence

Man is subject to insecurity. Animals need no justification. They are what they are, unquestionably. But man is different. Nature has

1. See L. Boros, *Im Menschen Gott begegnen* (Mainz, 1969, pp. 70 ff; Eng. trans.: *Meeting God in Man*, London, 1970).

delivered him over to insecurity, ordained him for unique adventure. Whereas the lower grades of life are driven inexorably onwards, the entire evolutionary plan changes in man. Man is impelled by goals, ideals, hopes and perceptions. On the surface of his existence he is, of course, also dependent on normal laws, orderly arrangements and groupings. He is inserted into a network of relationships in space, a network of events in time, a network of rules and regulations. Often he is simply a collection of pre-determined reactions, of opinions and values that have been imposed on him.

But behind all this there lies concealed a free and original spirit, constantly bursting out of its framework and aware of a future that is "not yet". At this level of his life man is deeply insecure and lonely. He is looking for a positive law of life. Here men give each other the food of the law of life, treating each other as brothers. Placed at the loneliest peak of natural development, man can do no more than step out into the dark, knowing that he is accompanied by others. His longing drives him onwards, out into the depths where there are no banks. He can only strain endlessly forward, far beyond the reality of his present life. Man has never grown used to his own destiny. His confidence always deserts him.[2]

If we are honest, we must admit that we can only penetrate the outer shell of our own selves; soon the unknown takes over. Perhaps we have been helpful to someone. But we can see only the immediate context. On such and such a day I gave him such and such. We can go deeper, however, and ask why we did so. Because he was in genuine need, and we wanted to save him from it. But is that all that happened? Looking still more closely we begin to understand that this was not the whole story by any means. For we were counting on support from him later on in such and such circumstances. Now we are beginning to penetrate even more deeply. And we see that what we did was out of vanity, because we wanted to make a good impression. But perhaps the moment comes—in the early morning maybe, when we are half asleep, and things can

2. Cf. M. Buber, *Einsichten* (Wiesbaden, 1953), p. 51.

57

sometimes seem curiously transparent, because self-assertion is not yet at work—when we perceive in a blinding flash that we really did it out of revenge, because we wanted to humiliate the other. But good can also come out of it—the wish to abolish an injustice; the unspoken hope of good to come; a love that does not yet dare to put itself into words . . . And so we begin to understand, to penetrate more and more deeply into, ourselves. But we never come to the ultimate reason. Before that happens we lose ourselves in darkness.[3]

That was only a small example. But it is like this everywhere in life, and everywhere it is uniquely different. To be thrown into uncertainty, into the pressure of necessary daring—this is man's essential destiny.[4]

From this modest beginning we now want to lay bare, piece by piece, the measure of human friendship, to the point where—"being together" ultimately changes into the experience of God.

It is Good that You are Here!

What is the meaning of this longing for human certainty? Does man perhaps want to see himself justified in the eyes of his fellows for his actions and decisions? Does he seek refuge from himself in another human being? Does he want him to help bear his responsibility? Does he want another human being to be with him in his difficult hours? All this may be true, and can play an important part in human relationships. But it is not the essence of the experience to which we give the name "friendship".

Let us imagine a "pure" friendship. Two people meet each other and are moved by each other. We are speaking of good people with no impure intentions. An immediate involvement occurs, a feeling of helpfulness and loyalty. One of these two people may start to ponder—What do I love in my friend? Is it his presence? Perhaps.

3. See R. Guardini, *Johanneische Botschaft* (Freiburg i. Br., 1962, pp. 81 f).
4. Cf. P. Wust, *Ungewissheit und Wagnis*.

I am happy when we are together. His face is beautiful, he is familiar to me, spending time with him is pleasant. But behind these appearances there is something deeper. This brother of mine also has human depths, out of which he speaks. But not even this is what really draws me to him. His innermost being reveals something still deeper. This man is a totality, built up from within according to an inner law of development. Beyond natural inwardness there is a spiritual depth that is filled with natural imagery, rich in temperament and vision, full of a selfless openness. It lies hidden in his mind where intellectual activity takes place. There we know truth, and the world around us grows clear. We can think in silence, and also, suddenly, let intuitive knowledge rise to the surface of our minds. And again—our spiritual depth is part of, and borne up by, something still deeper, by the depths of the person himself. This man means well by me. He will not make use of my liking for him; he will not use it for his own purposes.

All this, and much besides, would have to be said if one wanted to explain the seemingly insignificant sentence—It is good, that you are here! The "I" only becomes real in its relation to the "you". It was a time of indescribable joy. And then—great misfortune came. Your beautiful life was beset by trials and disruptions.

Your face became ugly, your charms were destroyed. People withdrew from you. But I remained with you, because I recognized that none of this touched on the essence of our friendship. Your life's strength ebbed away, bit by bit. Your body's harmony was destroyed. But my love did not grow less; indeed, it grew greater, the more you seemed to change. Your feelings became opaque, your moods precarious. You were no longer able to receive new impressions. I entered with you into your destruction, because none of this touched my relationship with you. Your thought became troubled and dark; you could no longer bring light into the world. You closed yourself even to me. You became angry, began to hate men, no longer saw the needs of others, could no longer even suffer from the fact that you had become angry. But my love for you grew still greater. To all appearances your life became "godless". Denial of God entered the innermost depths of you. In the end you could no longer endure even me, and drove me far away from your inner self. You now think me far from you. But I love you more than before.

It is always the same love. Perhaps purer, more understanding, more suffering, but always the same. You no longer possess anything, but you are you. You are my other self. In our happiness my love was unconditionally yours. You have always been more than your appearance. The self which I love and shall always love is no longer at your own disposal. But you have not lost anything. I preserve all your beauty in myself and give it to Him who joined us both together.

So now let us ask—Why can love last longer than the loss of every other excellence? Perhaps the answer is this—Because in friendship two people have become one not only by enriching each other, but to the very depths of their being. In every honestly experienced friendship there is present a mysterious third, a towering figure transcending every defect in the friendship—God. It is He who makes possible the uninterrupted love of two frail human beings. He is the reason why, in the beautiful words of Aristotle, a friendship that could one day cease has never been a real friendship at all. Let us try to go still further here.

To Love means to say—You will not Die

Friendship as the union of two selves lies beyond happiness or unhappiness. It is simply the other side of our life, and thus free from all danger. It confers immortality upon the beloved being—or perhaps this is simply the act of despairing love, thinking—It cannot be that you will leave me for ever. It cannot be that you are given over to eternal destruction. It cannot be that there can never again be the possibility of your developing into that which I saw in moments of inner vision.

If we think of a dead friend, our throat constricts with sadness. Perhaps we were never truly "present" to him; perhaps we never understood him correctly but judged him according to conventions and moods. Often we looked on him with the eyes of strangers and did not give him the possibility of being truly "himself". But precisely at such moments we experienced a secret consolation. There existed and exists for him a friend for eternity. Our broken friendship, our inner seeking, has always been an earthly expression of divine love. That is where he went, and from there he sends consoling words.

All is well. And so faith in the immortality of the loved one is not so much the result of logical deduction as the inner evidence of friendship itself. We must in all honesty place ourselves in these extreme situations, so that we can see the spirit of friendship emerge in them. In human friendship there is an archetypal proof that needs no further proof for him who loves—the presence of the friend, the opportunity of a limitless unfolding before him, and the presence of the Absolute which makes all this possible. This proof is criticized on all sides, and cannot defend itself. But precisely for this reason it is independent of superficial formulations and explanations. If, however, the beginnings of understanding are faithfully nourished, they will grow and penetrate our life. Friendship makes clear the unshakeable, soul-shattering presence of absolute goodness.[5]

And so there begins to grow in our life the practice of friendship. Man has found a new security in life through friendship. The greedy hold of selfishness begins to loosen. Man becomes calm, still, peaceful. He becomes attentive and courteous; dignified in his relations with others, understanding of human arrogance. He turns into a person who tries to hurt no one. He carefully avoids anything that could bring unpleasantness or disagreement into his surroundings—the clash of opinions, conflicting feelings, sadness and suspicion. He is concerned to make human life in the world pleasant and homelike. He cares for his surroundings. He is especially tender

5. See G. Marcel, *Présence et Immortalité* (Paris, 1959).

towards the timid, especially charming to the shy. He does not put himself into the limelight, says little about himself. He does not listen to gossip, does not dwell on insults. He is patiently aware of his neighbour's helplessness. He even tries to understand his enemy and is too large-hearted to allow others to be made fun of. With simple words he is able to console the oppressed, to understand the despairing, to make peace between two opponents, to forgive insults.[6]

How easy all this sounds. How simple and easy such an attitude seems to be. It is in these insignificant acts that the human heart shows itself to be possessed by God. Paul explained what happens here: "Blessed be the God and Father of our Lord Jesus Christ, the Father of mercies and God of all comfort, who comforts us in our afflictions, so that we may be able to comfort those who are in any affliction, with the comfort with which we ourselves are comforted by God" (2 Cor. 1. 3–4). Thus we can see how friendship opens up the human soul, the source of all friendliness. To experience this is the grace of God.

I Hope for Myself in You

To experience God's presence in earthly friendship and to be friendliness oneself—that is the dialectic which rules the good man's life. Such a man hopes for nothing for himself. Ultimately he is indifferent to what happens to his own life. But he pulls himself together in order to hope for himself also. The longing to surrender himself is the meaning of his life. Such was the moving experience of the man who so burnt with zeal and was so sorely tried, the man through whom the early Church came to self-awareness—the Apostle Paul.[7] He was a man who in one deeply felt

6. Cf. J. H. Newman, *The Idea of a University* (London, 1952, pp. 208–11).

7. J. H. Newman called Paul a friend of human nature, and developed this idea of him in one of his most beautiful sermons, "St Paul's gift of sym-

moment of his life experienced the mysterious oneness of Christ with his human brothers. On the way to Damascus it was revealed to him that the ultimate depth of human life was Christ himself (Acts 9. 3–4). To this overpowering presence whom he called "Spirit" (2 Cor. 3. 17) he dedicated his life. "Spirit" signifies for Paul in this context the reality of Christ himself (in his fullness and glory). An indescribable tension arose in his life. On the one hand he wished to "depart and be with Christ", on the other the self-same experience of Christ urges him to remain with his fellow-men (Phil. 1. 23–24). And thus he enters into the suffering of human limitation.

He is a sick man, a damaged being who carries his "treasure in earthen vessels" (2 Cor. 4. 7). He is oppressed on all sides, but does not complain. He is "perplexed, but not driven to despair" (2 Cor. 4. 8). He is "unskilled in speaking" and lacks "knowledge" (2 Cor. 11. 6). He has been "a fool" (2 Cor. 12. 11) who can rejoice that his strength is not his own, and who is glad of his sufferings, "knowing that suffering produces endurance" (Rom. 5. 3). He talks of his sufferings again and again: "You yourselves know how I lived among you all the time from the first day that I set foot in Asia, serving the Lord with all humility and with tears and with trials" (Acts 20. 19). Or again: "We do not want you to be ignorant, brethren, of the affliction we experienced in Asia; for we were so utterly, unbearably crushed that we despaired of life itself" (2 Cor. 1. 8). But he went on out of goodness, "strengthening the souls of the disciples, exhorting them to continue in the faith, and saying that through many tribulations we must enter the kingdom of God" (Acts 14. 22).

His farewell address at Miletus shows how close he was to his disciples: "He knelt down and prayed with them all. And they all wept and embraced Paul and kissed him, sorrowing most of all

---

pathy" (*Sermons preached on various Occasions*, Sermon VIII). See also M. G. Carroll, *The Mind and Heart of St Paul* (Langley, 1959).

because of the word he had spoken, that they should see his face no more. And they brought him to the ship" (Acts 20, 36–38). Warm friendship followed him everywhere. His companion, Titus, was very dear to him. He even sends advice about diet to another friend, Timothy (1 Tim. 5. 23). He cares most movingly for the young man who went to sleep during his speech and fell from the window (Acts 20. 9–12). He "rejoices" at the coming of three friends (1 Cor. 16. 17) and pleads on behalf of a Christian slave (letter to Philemon). Paul is grieved when people leave him, like Demas (2 Tim. 4. 10). He is glad when a friend visits him in Rome (2 Tim. 1. 16–17). At the end he was very much alone. Only Luke, the "beloved physician" (Col. 4. 14) still remained with him (2 Tim. 4. 11).

He calls on Timothy again and again to visit him. He feels he is near death: "I long night and day to see you, that I may be filled with joy" (2 Tim. 1. 4). "Do your best to come before winter" (2 Tim. 4. 21). Human and divine elements are mingled in this human soul, in a way that enables Paul to understand the mystery of Christ's humanity: "The meekness and gentleness of Christ" (2 Cor. 10. 1). His was a most moving life.

We have tried in these four chapters to show how human life is dependent on friendship. In the encounter with the unique being of another, man comes into contact with the transcendental, is inwardly changed and begins to be a witness to God. Man is the being that can experience God's presence in human friendship and can make friendship into a reality, witnessing to His presence. Once again human experience tries to depict this basic reality of human existence in the tightly-knit, delicately told story of the friendship between David and Jonathan.

On the one side there was the noble son of the king, Jonathan. As a young commander in the field, he had started Israel's fateful war. He killed the chief of the Philistines, led his men in surprise attacks, was deeply loved by the people so that they defended him even against his own father. He is honourable towards his friends, honest in the conduct of his life, externally already very winning. On the other side is David, a fairly plain shepherd boy, lively and fearless, sent by God to dethrone Saul, the father of Jonathan. David is a character of explosive contradictoriness, who can sing, dance and rejoice, but also pursues his goals with cunning and deceit. His soul is gripped by holiness. At the same time he can break commandments violently. The Bible describes four encounters between these two seemingly opposed human beings. In a situation of battles, uprisings, hatred, brutality and enthusiasm, we are confronted by a profound human story of inner involvement with God.

The first encounter between these two (1 Sam. 18. 1–4) took place after David's victory over Goliath. Saul summons the young shepherd boy and questions him. Jonathan is present, listening: "When he had finished speaking to Saul, the soul of Jonathan was knit to the soul of David, and Jonathan loved him as his own soul. And Saul took him that day, and would not let him return to his father's house. Then Jonathan made a covenant with David, because he loved him as his own soul. And Jonathan stripped himself of the robe that was upon him, and gave it to David, and his armour, and even his sword and his bow and his girdle." It is deeply moving how simple words can express the beginnings of human friendship. The sudden upsurge of attraction, the powerful emotion in the innermost depths of the soul, the altered way of life, Jonathan's present as symbol of self-giving, which incidentally reminds me of Rudolf Borchardt's poem beginning with the lines—

> What one wants one cannot give,
> One gives only what one must.
> Thus, one gives a kiss
> But one would like to give one's life.

The second encounter takes place in secret. David is fleeing from Saul, who wants to kill him. A heavy sadness falls on the two friends (1 Sam. 20. 42–42; 21. 1): "David rose from beside the stone heap and fell on his face to the ground, and bowed three times; and they kissed one another, and wept with one another until David recovered himself. Then Jonathan said to David, "Go in peace, forasmuch as we have sworn both of us in the name of the Lord, saying, 'The Lord shall be between me and you, and between my descendants and your descendants, for ever.' And he arose and departed; and Jonathan went into the city." In the heavy trials of the two friends, the inner reality, the mystery, of friendship emerges clearly. God unites them in friendship, and that is why their friendship cannot be destroyed. Man here is touching on something holy. Attraction changes to reverence. The two friends help each other as far as they can—they weep with each other. And in this way they confirm their friendship before the face of God.

The third encounter (1 Sam. 23. 15–18) between David, become leader of his men, and the king's son, is of a simple grandeur. Jonathan recognizes David's destiny and has decided to withdraw. He only wants to be "next" to him. The humility of friendship is shown here:—"David was afraid because Saul had come out to seek his life. David was in the wilderness of Ziph at Horesh. And Jonathan, Saul's son, rose, and went to David at Horesh, and strengthened his hand in God. And he said to him, 'Fear not; for the hand of Saul my father shall not find you; you shall be king over Israel, and I shall be next to you; Saul my father also knows this.' And the two of them made a covenant before the Lord; David remained at Horesh, and Jonathan went home."

The fourth occasion (2 Sam. 1. 17–27) is not a meeting, but David's lament at Jonathan's death; for Jonathan had been killed in the terrible carnage on Mount Gilboa, together with his father and his brothers. In his grief David once more experiences the beauty of his friendship with Jonathan: "Thy glory, O Israel, is slain . . . The bow of Jonathan turned not back . . . Jonathan, beloved and lovely . . . I am distressed for you, my brother Jonathan . . . Your love to me was wonderful, passing the love of women." The memory of pure love will continue to remain with David, a bond transcending death (see 2 Sam. 9. 1; 21. 7).

There is not much to say about friendship that we cannot learn from this story. Here it becomes perhaps even more clear than in other experiences of God how the human spirit is directed towards the Absolute, but experiences this Absolute as human destiny.[8] The idea of God is included in every honest human liking—the reality of a God whom Paul in one of the boldest statements of his passionate, God-loving soul, described as the "loving kindness" of God (Tit. 3. 4) and to whom man can speak as to a friend:

> Who is a God like thee, pardoning iniquity
>   and passing over transgression . . .
> He does not retain his anger forever
>   because he delights in steadfast love,
> He will again have compassion upon us,
>   he will tread our iniquities underfoot.
> Thou wilt cast all our sins
>   into the depths of the sea.
>
> (Micah 7. 18–29)

God is "steadfast love and faithfulness" (Ex. 34. 6); He is "merciful and gracious" (Ps. 103. 8).

God's friendship extends not only to men but to all things. "The compassion of the Lord is for all living beings" (Sir. 18. 13). In the prophet Hosea God offers His grace to men like a marriage gift, so that men can answer God in free surrender and learn to pass on the love that has been bestowed on them (Hosea 2. 21; 4. 1; 6. 4, 6; 10. 12). Man is confronted by a promise, a new world, which unfolds itself in the tenderness of God and is experienced as a saved world, in which God is "everything to everyone" (1 Cor. 15. 28).

> Let me hear what the Lord will speak
>   for he will speak peace to his people . . .
>   that glory may dwell in our land.

8. See the explanation by H. Urs von Balthasar of "berit", "chesed", "chen", "rahamim", "sedek", "sedeka", "mispat", "emet", "emuna" and "shalom" as "God made present" in *Herrlichkeit*, vol. III, 2 (Einsiedeln, 1967; pp. 138–64).

Steadfast love and faithfulness will meet;
   righteousness and peace will kiss each other.
Faithfulness will spring up from the ground,
   and righteousness will look down from the sky.
Yea, the Lord will give what is good,
   and our land will yield its increase.

(Ps. 85. 8–12)

This new world, lit by God's friendship, has already broken through in Christ—whose existence was basically only the revelation that "God is love" (1 John 4. 8–16)—and in the continuous affirmation of our humanity, the unequalled fulfilment of the word God spoke at the beginning of the world to the entire creation: "It is good that you are" (cf. Gen. 1. 13).

Is not such a picture of God and men one-sided? Are not God's hard demands weakened thereby? Is not the mystery of God hidden even more behind human perception? The man who asks these questions is apparently unaware of the demands made by love as self-giving. Its ultimate demands do not lie in God's commandments but in the love he has put into our hearts (Rom. 5. 5), by which we are ruled (2 Cor. 5. 14), and from which nothing can any longer separate us (Rom. 8. 35–39). This is perhaps the hardest but also the most joy-making demand of our faith—to be witness to God's friendship in an often hate-filled and for this reason unhappy world. "Friendship, this gift of God in us—let us only speak good of it."9

9. This was the advice of a clever and holy Dominican Provincial in England to one of his brethren, whose conscience was troubled because of a human friendship. Cited in Evelyn Waugh's *The Life of Ronald Knox* (London, 1959), p. 125.

5. Helpful Man

WHEN the Apostle Peter had to talk for the first time to non-believers about Christ, he was obviously embarrassed. How was he to tell them in a few sentences about the overwhelming experience of the last years, which united him with Christ for ever? Hesitantly and seeking for the right words, he begins his speech. With difficulty he describes the secret of his heart. In unassuming words he tells them that Christ "went about doing good" (Acts 10. 38). There is not perhaps a great deal of theology here, nevertheless the words move us with their sense of immediacy. The listeners get some inkling of what lies hidden behind them. Perhaps it is this: At last there has come into the world a perfectly good man. Then pain fills the Apostle's soul as he tells them: "They put him to death by hanging him on a tree" (Acts 10. 39). Finally he announces the victory of the good man: "God raised him on the third day" (Acts 10. 40).

It is the very baldness and unpretentiousness of this speech that reveals the essence of the astonishing mystery of Christ. We find it most difficult to speak of that which fills our soul the most. But the Apostle's emotion communicates itself and enters into the soul of his listeners. What happens is that transformation of life in which man becomes a Christian. "While Peter was still saying this, the Holy Spirit fell on all who heard the word" (Acts 10. 44). We do not want to analyse this event further here, but only to use it as an introduction to our next thought—that *active goodness is where God is encountered*. The words are unassuming, and what they are saying could easily be missed through familiarity.

Human life depends on goodness. What is the meaning of

goodness in life? Let us first look at our own life, its indecision and muddle-headedness. What do we find there?

First—our life is divided into days. It is fragmented in time. Days come and go. Indeed they go almost as soon as they have come. They seem to carry along with them a rush of things and events. And with these a part of our life goes too. It is not simply something external that disappears, but that "outside" of ourselves that we are constantly striving to turn inwards. We change the things in our life. We experience their goodness and their fullness, they become part of our life. And then, suddenly, they are no longer there and leave behind them an almost unbearable emptiness.[1] This emptiness we seek again and again to fill with that strange and often bitterly disappointing element that we call the possession of things. Man picks out a piece of the word, presses it to his heart, and for the moment feels himself fulfilled. But each such fulfilment further constricts his life. It is easy enough to see how many things escape us, since we pay attention to only a few. And we cannot even hold on to these few for ever.[2]

Thus the obstinate drive towards enrichment continues to be active in us, a hunger for experience, a longing for a life that is both more and different. Then suddenly man notices how strange everything has become for him, how little closeness and warmth he has known. He begins to look upon himself with the eyes of a stranger. What is this being that is filled by a multitude of things and yet is empty, that is driven by longing, yet is nowhere at home?[3] Man is possessed by alien elements which have pulled his life apart.[4] He

1. The following refer primarily to Aurelius Augustinus. See the present writer's article, "Les Catégories de la Temporalité chez Saint Augustin" (*Archives de Philosophie*, July–September 1958, pp. 323 ff). Cf. *Enarrationes in Psalmos* 38; 7 (PL 36, 419); 121; 6 (PL 37, 1623); 62; 6 (PL 36, 752).

2. Cf. *De vera religione* 20; 40 (PL 34, 139); *Sermones* 124, 2; 2 (PL 38, 687); *De vera religione* 22; 43 (PL 34, 140); *Sermones* 331, 1; 1 (PL 38, 1459).

3. Cf. *Sermones* 125; 11 (PL 38, 698); *De libero arbitrio* III, 7; 21 (PL 32, 1281).

4. Cf. *Confessiones* XI, 26; 33 (BT 287); XI, 29; 39 (BT 292).

is nowhere truly himself. He looks into his soul only for brief moments, seeing a broken reflection of things and of fleeting feelings, experiences and awarenesses—events that belong to him but are no part of his enduring and total self.[5] A rich poverty and a poor richness—St Augustine thus defines life as "*ek*-sistence", as a standing apart, as fragmentation.[6]

Thus in essence there is no being that is totally itself, realizing all it possesses within itself. And death is not the external completion of a being, but the inwardly present culmination of its experiences and encounters. Human life is not simply a "running towards death" but a "living towards and in death".[7] As "viator", wayfarer, man's life is forever in transit. Man is constantly on the way, a wanderer, a journeyman, a pilgrim or simply tramp. The symbolism of the "Way" does not signify a "moving straight towards a goal" but the often fruitless effort of trying to find such a goal. Our ways are seldom anything other than tracks leading to nowhere.[8] "We are not yet. We hope to be."[9] "The reality in man is never attained, is always in expectation."[10] Thus our life is not simply "expectation", but more exactly and radically, an "expectation of expectations, which themselves await their expectation."[11] This is the "sickness unto death" that is part of every human life, and of which Augustine and Kierkegaard could speak so

5. Cf. *Enarrationes in Palmos* 121; 6 (PL 37, 1623): 121, 9 (PL 37, 1624).

6. Cf. *De vera religione* 21; 41 (PL 34, 139); *Sermones* 125; 11 (PL 38, 698).

7. Cf. the "concept" of death in M. Heidegger's *Sein und Zeit*. See too St Augustine, *Sermones* 97, 3; 3 (PL 38, 590); *De Divitate Dei* 13; 10 (CCL 48, 392); *In Joannem* 38; 10 (CCL 36, 343); *Confessiones* IV, 10; 15 (BT 65); *Enarrationes in Psalmos* 127; 15 (PL 37, 1686).

8. *Enarrationes in Psalmos* 76; 3–4 (PL 36, 972); 39; 3 (P; 36, 434); 129; 1 (PL 37, 1696). See too M. Heidegger, *Holzwege* (Frankfurt, a.M., 1957).

9. B. Pascal, *Pensées*, no. 172.

10. E. Bloch, *Das Prinzip Hoffnung* (Frankfurt a.M., 1959), vol. 1, p. 285.

11. J. P. Sartre, *L'Etre et le Néant* (Paris, 1943), p. 622; Eng. trans.: *Being and Nothingness*).

71

movingly.[12] It is in truth a struggle for life, a despairing attempt
to retain, to unfold and to communicate what is most real and
beautiful in our life, a battle with "unequal weapons", indeed
often without any weapons at all, simply with naked hands
struggling against an enemy whom one does not know and does
not see.[13]

A life that has been internally poisoned by feelings, aversion,
enmity and hatred is one that we feel more and more to be a prison,
from which there is no escape.[14] "Growing old" as a fact of our
existence becomes more and more certain—a narrowing and
hardening of life within, a constriction of the feelings.[15] Our life
becomes unfruitful soil, a wilderness of passion and sadness, unfit
to let new life grow.[16] Augustine uses a still more vivid symbolism,
that of decomposition. Disgust as the basic feeling of life is in no
way the discovery of modern existential anthropology.[17]

The sense of exile[18] fills the human soul with longing for its true
home, for an ultimate security,[19] for a situation where longing no
longer passes from "expectation to expectation";[20] for a life of

12. *Sermones* 97, 3; 3 (PL 38, 590); *Enarrationes in Psalmos* 102; 6 (PL 37,
1320); Sermones 17, 7 (PL 38, 128). See also Kierkegaard's *Sickness unto
Death.*

13. *De civitate Dei* 21; 15 (CCL 48, 781); *Sermones* 344; 1 (PL 39, 1512);
De agone christiano 2; 2 (CV 41, 103); *Enarrationes in Psalmos* 142; 16 (PL 37,
1854); 49; 22 (PL 36, 579); 13 (PL 36, 523); 136; 7 (PL 37, 1765); 141; 17
(PL 37, 1843); 141; 17–18 (PL 37, 1843); 147; 5 (PL 37, 1917).

14. *Enarrationes in Psalmos* 141; 7 (PL 37, 1843); 67; 26 (PL 36, 830).

15. *Enarrationes in Psalmos* 131, 1 (PL 37, 1716); 47; 5 (PL 36, 536).

16. *Enarrationes in Psalmos* 91; 8 (PL 37, 1176); 76; 7 (PL 36, 974); 139;
11 (PL 37, 1809).

17. *Sermones* 254, 4; 5 (PL 38, 1184); 361, 9; 9 (PL 39, 1184).

18. *Enarrationes in Psalmos* 49; 22 (PL 36, 759); *Sermones* 124, 4; 4 (PL 38,
688); *Enarrationes in Psalmos* 148; 4 (PL 37, 1940).

19. *Enarrationes in Psalmos* 55; 9 (PL 36, 652; *Sermones* 49, 3; 3–4 (PL 38,
322); *De civitate Dei* XXII, 29; 6 (CCL 48, 862).

20. *In Joannem* 63; 1 (CCL 36, 485); *Enarrationes* in Psalmos 62; 16 (PL
36, 758); 104; 3 (PL 37, 1392); *De Trinitate* XV, 2; 2 (PL 42, 1059).

permanent safety in an eternal present eternally opened up.[21] Sometimes there occurs already in our earthly life a breakthrough to understanding and to safety,[22] which however cannot develop into permanence. Man continually falls back into the uncertainty of every day.[23] He is no longer astonished at the abberations of the human spirit because he sees his own life also as a curiously restricted one.[24] Pushed into an abyss of despair, locked into his own inability to communicate himself, uncertain in his heart,[25] man cries out, calls for help. In this cry his life continues to find an ultimate meaning.[26]

For suddenly the unexpected may happen, the inexplicable, in the dark context of the world. A person becomes present for us, one who is perhaps himself frail and stumbling about in the dark, and reaches out to us his helping hand. It may be that he has no answer himself, but his nearness warms our heart. Suddenly our chains fall, our fetters grow loose. A light shines out, and meaning re-enters our life. We are filled with astonishment. How does a man acquire the strength to open himself up to another's need and darkness, to rise above his own misery and burden himself with the burdens of another's life? How can a man who is himself broken by life help another human being? How can he make another's life easier? The

21. *De Doctrina christiana* 1, 38; 42 (PL 34, 42 (PL 34, 35)); *Epistulae* 130, 14; 17 (CV 44, 71–72); *De Civitate dei* XXII, 30; 1 (CCL 48, 862; *De civitate Dei* XII, 30; 5 (CCL 48, 866); *De Genesi ad litteram* IV, 13; 24 (CV 28, 1. 110).

22. *Confessiones* VII, 17; 23 (BT 146); VII, 10; 16 (BT 141); IX, 10; 24 (BT 200); *Enarrationes in Psalmos* 41; 10 (PL 36, 471).

23. *Enarrationes in Psalmos* 41, 10 (PL 36, 471); *Confessiones* X, 40; 65 (BT 259); VII, 17; 23 (BT 146).

24. *Enarrationes in Psalmos* 102; 6 (PL 37, 1320); *Contra ep. quam vocant fundamenti* 2 (CV 25, 194).

25. *Enarrationes in Psalmos* 41; 13 (PL 36, 473); 100; 12 (PL 37, 1292); 55; 9 (PL 36, 652); 134; 16 (PL 37, 1749); *Sermones* 47, 14; 23 (PL 38, 312); 49, 3; 3 (PL 38, 321).

26. *Enarrationes in Psalmos* 39; 3 (PL 36, 434); 129; 1 (PL 37, 1696).

answer is quite simple—With words spoken into the darkness, to a stranger, and continually, faithfully repeated: "You are not alone."

Man always experiences the attempt to help as a transcendental event, as a breakthrough of absolute goodness into the darkness of the world, as a privileged encounter with the Absolute in his life. He always surrounds the act of helping with the halo of the miraculous. But the miraculous is explained by a deeper, more genuine reality, a more profound insight—namely that human life, despite all its appearances of darkness and bewilderment, is yet constantly upheld by God, safe in the goodness of his arms, at no time totally estranged from him. This knowledge is the profoundest miracle of our life—the unexpected that transcends all hope.

This can be clearly seen in that deeply human but mysterious event which we call the Christian prayer of petition. Man feels his own helplessness in face of the need of others. He sees the life and work of other men, to whom he is well disposed, indeed their eternal destiny, threatened by situations in the world which are not under his control. He sees them in danger of damnation. With the spontaneity of his heart he calls on the Absolute Being to intervene and remove this danger from them. But at the same time he knows that he has thereby placed himself in danger, too. He now finds himself on the edge of superstition, tempted to use the divine for human purposes. He knows that for the sake of another, he is darkening the image of the God in whom he seeks refuge, that he is calling on a God who does not exist. In a dialectical movement, he leaves the granting of his prayer to God's will: "Not my will be done but thine!" At this point he touches directly on the mystery. He recognizes that needs and sufferings which affect only the external life of man are basically unimportant and do not reach the reality of life. The essence lies elsewhere—in the knowledge that God is love. Fundamentally every prayer of petition is directed towards this one thing—I beg you, Lord, let this person inwardly experience that you are really love, that he has a refuge in you, that he is always at home in you. Let this insight be with him in all his needs and amidst everything that happens to him. Let him experience his sufferings, his losses and his hopelessness as resting in your love, which no one can take from him. Let him look at his perhaps inevitable need with new eyes, the eyes of your love. Give him the experience of your love and he will be able to go on with his life.

Thus the essence of the prayer of petition (and also the essence of divine Providence) consists in a change of the self. This is the fundamental miracle of life of which we spoke just now—the experience of the loving nearness of God and the living of our perhaps sorely tried life in this knowledge. Human help acquires real meaning only when it becomes a witness for others of the nearness of God. Here we come again to the point discussed earlier—that human helping cannot and should not be measured by its success, but only in the measure in which one's helpfulness is bound up with a selfless wish to be close and good to the other.

The image of helpful man and the corresponding human need for help is shown in the Bible by the life of the prophet Elisha. This man had a curious destiny, as told in the so-called Elisha cycle of the Second Book of Kings (chapters 2–13). One single section stands out in its vividness from all the rest. In the fourth chapter, amidst descriptions of chaos, hatred and revenge, there appears the man Elisha, towering over all confusions—the personification of human goodness. This goodness is shown in five quiet miracles which could just as well have been found in the Gospels—so clear, inward and human are they. Let us pause a moment and meditate on the "good man".

First. The Widow's Jar

The wife of "one of the sons of the prophets" asks for Elisha's help in a hopeless situation. "Your servant my husband is dead; and you know that your servant feared the Lord, but the creditor has come to take my two children to be his slaves." The woman had nothing in the house except a jar of oil. Elisha told her to borrow empty vessels, "and not too few", from her neighbours. Then she shut herself and her two sons into the house, and filled the empty vessels, one after the other, with oil, till none was left. And she sold the oil, paid her debts, and together with her sons lived on the proceeds of the rest (2 Kings 4. 1–7). If we consider the inner meaning of this simply told, fable-like story, we come to an extraordinarily deep insight.

Human life, limited and dangerous as it is, is nevertheless made for super-abundance. This plenitude of life, deeply desired by man and after its reception felt to be most truly his, is only given him in grace. Man has to hold himself in readiness for the gift of plenitude. The "empty vessels" resemble his own readiness to receive this grace, his gnawing dissatisfaction, the longing which belongs to his earthly life. What we are given here as background to the symbolic events is an image of a God Who exceeds all counting and calculation. It is a God who delights in giving; a God who not only loves, but whose whole being is love; who dares to let his goodness be communicated through his human brothers; a God, therefore, who descends into the narrowness of human life in a measure that perhaps exceeds all human understanding.

Since God "has" nothing that He can give, but "is" everything, He turns Himself from giver into gift. But his gift can only be complete when He Himself becomes our own receptiveness, when therefore our personal relationship with Him is so intensified that our being with Him becomes an eternal dialectic of fulfilment and ever-increasing receptiveness.

Here we come to a situation (as exemplified by the quick re-action of the listener, "Pity that the poor woman did not borrow more empty vessels"), in which the person begins to grow towards infinity in the fulfilment of his potentialities, and of the transcendence of this potentiality through this same fulfilment.

Now if human helpfulness is to be a sign of God's nearness, and if the true helpfulness of man consists in his being present for the other, then it follows that our nearness to the person we are helping must preserve and nourish the conviction that we are not helping him purely in his material and spiritual need, but that he is also receiving human love, that is, human presence. To discover how we can best bring this about, according to our own individual temperament, is the grace-inspired task of witnessing.

Second: The Unfruitful Pair

In the course of his wanderings, Elisha always visited a family who received him hospitably and looked after him well. In this house the often very tired prophet was surrounded by an atmosphere of helpful calm and friendliness. The husband and wife had made for him a small roof chamber, with a bed, a table, a chair and even a lamp. He could rest there whenever he passed by. But the couple had a secret sorrow. They had no son. And when the prophet was about to depart, he said to the woman: " 'At this season, when the time comes round, you shall embrace a son.' She replied, 'No, my lord, O man of God, do not lie to your maidservant.' But the woman conceived, and she bore a son about that time the following spring, as Elisha had said to her" (2 Kings 4. 8–17). Again we note the sparseness of the account, and how true it is to life. For many the birth of a son would not have signified anything extraordinary. But for this ageing couple, it was the fulfilment of a secret longing.

Barrenness in marriage symbolizes here, as elsewhere in the Bible, the emptiness of life as a whole. Into this emptiness God's nearness brings fulfilment. All of a sudden new life is produced, where before there was only sterility and nothingness. Man feels himself content. In the background is the image of a God of longing, for whom nothing is ultimately lost, and no source permanently dried up; a God for whom no human hopelessness is too great. It is the newly living and newly life-giving God.

God's love is mysteriously directed towards the unhappy who

are denied fulfilment. It includes the "pathos of being moved". In its eyes, the important ones are those that are helpless, the chosen one those whom the world has rejected. God's love is especially given to outsiders and strangers, and brings them fulfilment. It is they who are called blessed by the God who includes all men in his mercy. But love shows all men to be unhappy, and every life to be in some sense barren. It is precisely in periods of our perhaps hidden unhappiness that there are signs of the promise of life.

The most important help man can give to others, if he wants his helping to be a witness to God's love, is to spend his own life in this love. "The unhappy are the favourites of God." Thus he must show by his own life that, despite everything that happens, and precisely because it is as it is, he trusts in God. And in this way he once again makes visible the charismatic character of God's goodness. For nowhere else does our life become so truly our own as in our unhappiness, and in the attempt to look on life, nevertheless, with hope. Sometimes we shall live with quiet resignation, or fall silent before the inexplicable; at others we shall be quietly joyful at having known unhappiness and being able, therefore, to understand our unhappy brothers better in the light of this experience. And again we shall know what it is to be free of self and ready to be available for others.

At all events, our helpful nearness to the unhappy must always be, in one form or another, the nearness of a fellow-sufferer, but one who sees his own misfortune as a sign of God's presence. This enables us to understand the instinctive tendency of those saints who dared to imitate Christ in his sufferings, and whose lives opened up the world to God's mysterious love.

Third: The Awakening of a Child

The parents were happy to have given life to a bright and lively son. But one day the boy ran out to the field where his father was, among the reapers, and suddenly said to him, "Oh, my head, my head!"

78

The father had him carried to his mother and went back to work. "The child sat on her lap till noon, and then he died."

The first thought of the woman was—Elisha will help. So she set off and ordered the servant to urge the ass on quickly. When she arrived, she caught hold of the prophet's feet. Thereupon Elisha's servant wanted to turn her away, but the prophet prevented him, saying, "Let her alone, for she is in bitter distress; and the Lord has hidden it from me, and has not told me." Then Elisha heard the unhappy story and wished to send his servant with the miraculous staff in order to help the boy. But the woman was in despair and did not let go of Elisha, until he agreed to accompany her. The servant who had gone ahead did not succeed in raising the dead boy. Elisha himself went to the boy, shut the door, threw himself despairingly on the child, and prayed. "And the child opened his eyes." Elisha then summoned the mother and said, "Take up your son." She came, and fell at his feet, bowing to the ground; then she took up her son and went out (2 Kings 4. 18–37).

It is a message from a God who has "no pleasure in the death of anyone" (Ez. 18, 32) but gives his own life to his creation and holds our frail life in his hands, warming and nourishing it; a message from a God who not only lives and is alive, but whose very essence is "life" itself, life in which "what is mortal may be swallowed up" (2 Cor. 5. 4). Such an image of God is also the most far-reaching protest man can make against death as an end to life, as negation and punishment. Out of this tension between the reality of death and the God confronting it as enemy but seemingly powerless against it, there begins to grow in the human soul the awareness that death is the way to real life, our real birth therefore, and must somehow be seen as a proof of the living God's grace for us. All men must have the possibility of receiving life in its wholeness, in awareness, freedom, encounter. But for this man must break out of his darkness and self-imprisonment, must waken to real life, must enter into reality. What appears, in the story of Samuel, as a gift to a poor, sad woman is in actual fact a message of God's intention. How

God will bring about the victory over death is not yet made plain. But if man understands that God is love and life, he will no longer regard as strange the message of a God who has taken death upon himself to become the "Author of life" (Acts 3. 15). Indeed he will not regard as strange a God who performs other acts of life over and above the act of our salvation, until finally, despite human opposition and rejection, through an act of—to us—unimaginable self-humiliation, he brings all living things to their final consummation.

If one has heard the message of love and life, one will leave everything to Him calmly, quietly and with knowing heart. For He is "greater than our hearts" (1 John 3. 20), and his creative will knows no bounds. This is true, too, wherever we witness to Him by helping others in our unhappy world. Our nearness to our fellow-men, our experience of suffering and the love of God, shall become our witness to the reality of life and love. This too is how the primitive Church understood its vocation: "Go and stand in the temple and speak to the people all the words of this life" (Acts 5. 20).

Fourth: The Poisoned Food

Elisha once was with the "sons of the prophets" during a famine. He said to his servant, "Set out the great pot, and boil pottage for the sons of the prophets." One of them went out and plucked the gourd of a wild vine, and cut it up and put it into the pot. But when the men were given this food, they cried out, "O man of God, there is death in the pot!" So Elisha told them to bring him some "meal". And he put it into the pot and said, "Pour out for the men, that they may eat." And they found nothing bad any longer in the pot (2 Kings 4. 38–41). What a smilingly told—so I believe—story of a divine miracle. The explanation is this: The wild or bitter gourd (cucumis colocynthis) was even at that time a highly efficient purgative; it was only poisonous in large quantities.

We can explain the symbolism of these events by saying that God here shows us that He lets goodness prevail. He does not permit men to poison one another. For this is one of the greatest obstacles in our attempt to help others, since the world by and large shows little awareness of God's presence. How easy it is to create a poisonous atmosphere among a group of people so that they are in danger of being destroyed by it. It is usually a matter of quite trivial happenings—a word misunderstood, an unconsidered act, an unforgiven insult, a hard or hurtful expression—and at once the entire group life has been poisoned. A discrepancy arises between what is said and what is meant. We are suddenly powerless. Words are given different meanings and charged into their opposites. We no longer want to know the truth, only to be victorious in a meaningless battle of words. Hatred fills everyone, and they are no longer free, relaxed and still. In their wrought-up state they often turn on the innocent whom they feel they must torment in order to justify themselves. Small-mindedness, calculation, resentment and ill-fated self-pity descends on them all. An evil atmosphere pervades everything and they cannot free themselves of it.

When a truly good man, a quiet and pure spirit, gay and clear-sighted, finds himself amidst such confusion, the spell suddenly lifts. And we perceive the compulsive power of evil, and the triviality of the reasons that call it into being. We can no longer properly understand how we could have become involved in it all. We find we can breathe again and be calm and happy. Forgiveness is once more possible, and also mercy. The evil in us craves for nothing marvellous and spectacular, nothing at first glance remarkable (no "grievous" sins, no gigantic rebelliousness). It wants only to force us into dishonesty in small ways, and into hardness of heart, into a twilight existence in which we can no longer perceive truth, no longer believe in goodness, are no longer aware of the purity of good intentions and no longer capable of receiving love.[27]

27. This reminds one of C. S. Lewis' *That Hideous Strength*, where the author depicts the strange effectiveness of evil as twilight, change of perspective, and banality.

Thus help does not consist in impressive deeds but in personal witness of righteousness. This means—quietly, thoughtfully, in stillness and restraint, to open up the world to truth; to let light shine forth, in whose brightness things appear in their true nature and right proportions; to live a life in which everything is as it ought to be; to be modest and well disposed towards others in the way Paul describes so unforgettably: "Speaking the truth in love" (Eph. 4. 15).

Fifth: The Multiplication of Bread

Lastly, it is told of Elisha that "A man came from Ba'al-shal'ishah, bringing the man of God bread of the first fruits, twenty loaves of barley, and fresh ears of grain in his sack. And Elisha said, 'Give to the men, that they may eat.' But his servant said, 'How am I to set this before a hundred men?' So he repeated, 'Give them to the men that they may eat, for thus says the Lord, "They shall eat and have some left."' And he set it before them. And they ate, and had some left, according to the word of the Lord" (2 Kings 4. 42–44).

From the language and the form of the words it can be seen that this text is fragmentary. There is no introduction, nothing is set up or developed. But the Christian who reads this story in the perspective of the miracle of Christ's multiplication of bread (Mt. 14. 13–21; Mk 6. 31–44; Luke 9. 10–17; John 6. 1–15; and also Mt. 15. 32–39; Mark 8. 1–10), that is to say, in the Johannine understanding of propotype and promise of the bread of life, which is the reality of Christ, will find great wealth of meaning there. He will see a God who transforms the world, who does not directly break into our life but takes note of what is already present, accepts it, multiplies and changes it. The real mystery, however, lies in the person of the unknown man and the twenty loaves of barley, or in John in the equally unknown boy who has five barley loaves and two fish (John 6. 9). Here we see clearly God's way of acting. In His marvellous modesty He uses His creatures, and lets them inwardly grow. From the beginning of creation He constantly produces new causes, and increases and transcends man's powers in order to enable the world to unfold from within itself, and the "less" to become a "more"; to enable the world to grow right up to the birth of man, and through man to that transcendental, absolute "more" that is God Himself. In the stillness, in the pliable depths of the world, God works in souls, in attitudes and states of mind, and not through domination and acts of power. If the world were here to teach us about God, God's glory would shine out everywhere in her, inextinguishably. But the world is not a demonstration of God's power, but a personal example of His love and restraint.

The man who helps others truly witnesses to God whenever he so transcends human need that his fellow-sufferers notice nothing or almost nothing of it. This is true helpfulness—to enable another to find the way out for himself in order to accomplish deeds of which he had previously felt himself incapable. By "unnoticed giving" man most closely resembles God's eternal goodness.[28] It is the graciousness of God shining out in human selflessness.

Summing up, we can say that a person who, with still modesty, keeping himself in the background, reaches out a helping hand to his fellows, whose very nearness radiates an abundance of love, who is willing to be with others in their helplessness, who rouses them to new life, whose very existence is evidence for them of the existence of truth—and who, finally, does not force his help on them but lets it grow out of themselves—such a person reveals to us the presence of God in the world. And this is so even when he does not speak to us of God, or perhaps does not himself know God, and may have to say in embarrassment to the God, whose image and likeness he has become through his charity, "Lord, when did I do all this?" (cf. Mt. 25. 37–40). Here we have perhaps the fourth

28. See the exposition on the "anonymity of God" in H. Urs von Baltha-sar's *Herrlichkeit* (vol. 1, Johannes-Verlag, Einsiedeln 1961; pp. 464 f) and the passages cited there from Pascal.

definition of human existence—Man is that being who, in helpful nearness, becomes the image and witness of God for men.

The man who truly helps others is close to God. He is very close to that saving God who embraces us in our exile, who receives the beggar, who pulls the drowning towards himself, who is the God of all the broken, outlawed and lost; the God who blesses even our misfortunes; who descended into the terrible depths of the human soul and faced the dark shadow of death for our sakes; the God of those who are given over to loneliness, the God who tenderly loves the least of us and the most hopeless; the God of unembittered yet supplicating love. When we use the word "saints", we tend to think of exceptional cases. But in the light of our meditation we should rather think of saints as those who want to be like everybody else in the desire of their hearts—who are in love with life, who give hope to others, who help and console them. Saints are people whose nearness bring balm to the soul of their brothers.

If we honestly ask ourselves what in our life has remained most beautiful, enduring and bliss-making, we need not answer quietly and modestly, "Of all that once was ours, there has remained only what we have wasted and given away.[29]

29. G. von Le Fort, *Gedichte* (Wiesbaden, 1958), p. 17; "Gnade des Dichters". "Oh fold your wings for me, my songs, you familiar figures. Pray oh pray for me and lovingly surround me with all your treasures, once my own—My soul lends me the life I gave you only for an hour, only an hour can I survive, for oh, all that belonged to me has been squandered and given away."

6. Protected Man

EVERY human being bears within himself something that needs "protecting", something he wants to guard from the rush and pressures of the world. Frequently it is something delicate, precious and lovely, which for this very reason does not belong into the sphere of public life. For it would break into pieces there.

Often it is recollections of special moments in his life, of sufferings endured and shy longings. These lie deeply buried, sunk within our innermost being, and only occasionally, when we are meditating, and are carried out of ourselves, do they emerge from the depths of our memory. The appearance of a long-forgotten landscape, the likeness of a dead friend, a colour, a sound, a human face—these are sunken "islands"[1] that suddenly rise up out of the sea of our forgetfulness, are briefly present, then disappear again and once more appear. One stays with them, dreams one's life into them, and feels quite at home there, in the regions of the purely personal, the inward and the no longer communicable.

But there is also special knowledge that we must protect—knowledge that would disintegrate in the harsh light of every day, unable to defend itself against its pressures. Nevertheless this knowledge is more important, more vital for us than all other superficial insights the world can give us. One thinks, for example, of the knowledge that the kingdom of heaven belongs to the poor in spirit, that mourners will one day find sure consolation, that the

1. See R. J. Humm, *Die Inseln* (Zürich, 1968). For an evaluation of this important book, see the discussion in the *Neue Zürcher Zeitung*, Sunday, November 10th 1968; foreign edition no. 309, p. 49).

meek will inherit the land; that the mild possess tne world, in its reality and its depths; that it is good to hunger and thirst after justice, to be of pure heart, to be merciful and bring peace.

Often too we have experiences of exceptional fragility—experiences in prayer, hidden sympathy for our fellow-men, awareness of a unique destiny that is ours or of inescapable need, intuitive understanding of music and poetry. None of this can be shouted out to the world; all of it must therefore be carefully guarded. In these situations man turns to his inner self, feels himself at home there, and comes truly alive. Everything else in life can then be put aside—experienced, communicated, understood and fulfilled equally well by others. But not this inward, delicate, frail and uncommunicable thing. The thesis we want to put forward here is that man can experience the nearness of God with special intensity in these protected areas of his life; indeed that they are directly related to the presence of God.

Which are the aspects of life that we instinctively want to protect in this way? If we exclude for the moment those areas of life that deserve special consideration, like sickness, persecution, imprisonment, sadness and so on, and confine ourselves only to those that essentially need safeguarding, then we must name—the child, the woman and the old. These stand for certain necessary attitudes to life, if man wants to be fully alive. They are symbols of immediacy, of tenderness and of light.

The Child: Immediacy

What is the meaning of the sadness that takes hold of us whenever we think back on our childhood, whenever a word, a taste, a tone of voice or an image calls it back into our minds? It is the feeling of having lost something for ever, something that we shall never possess again. It is true that we have all as children had our problems and difficulties; we were seized by strange feelings of rebellion and revenge. Days, weeks, even whole stages of our childhood were poisoned. But these are not the things that we miss today, and which fill our minds with longing for a new childhood.

What we should like to rediscover is the immediacy of experience that is the essential characteristic of childhood. A child's soul can be completely enthralled by happenings, things and feelings, so that it no longer looks inwards at itself but loses itself in contemplation of the other. The totality of itself, undivided and unfragmented, comes very close to the totality of the other. It makes no calculations; it justifies nothing, conceals nothing. It is simply "there" with wide-open eyes, caught in an overwhelming experience, in a mood of heightened awareness of which it is not even aware.

This gives us an indication of the profound meaning contained in the comparison, often alas made sentimentally, of children and "angels". It is not true, of course, that the angels of revelation were pretty, cute little creatures. Quite the contrary. But in one thing children do resemble them—in the intensity of their life, which Rilke describes in the poetic words—Angels are "Tumulte stürmisch entzückten Gefühls".[2] Angels not only experience raptures of transport—they are rapture itself: self-surrender in self-forgetfulness. Their whole being is caught up in the one cry—"Holy, holy, holy." They do not reason or ask questions, but are pure feeling. In this children resemble angels.

When a simple man speaks about children, the word "paradise" comes naturally to his tongue. Thus once again we get this feeling of unhealthy sentimentality, but it is quite untrue that the powerful and moving situation which we know as man's unfallen state, and from which he fell to his present fallenness, was a matter of dreams and carefree twilight living. It could be that the human race had never been in greater danger than at that point in its history, never more at risk, never more plagued by the harshnesses of life. Nevertheless everything was "different". This difference did not come from the world, which was the same world as now, except that it was even more harsh and threatening. The difference came from

2. "Riots of rapturous delight" (translator).

God, because it was from him that man knew the world, in a deep, as yet non-verbal and unarticulated, but all-embracing knowledge of his mystery. Here we get once again the aspect of "directness", of self-forgetful surrender, in which we recognized the constituent elements of child-life.

The life of the child lies extended between paradise and the angelic world, but not in a sentimental sense. It is illumined by the metaphysical aspects of these three states of being. In this sense we can also understand why the child "as child" is endangered and requires protection. It is constantly given over to "visions", and throws itself with all the undividedness of its experience into the illumined Presence, making it part of its own life. Something similar may have occurred in the course of the events which Christian theology gives as the cause of the disordered nature of our world—the fall of the angels and the original sin of mankind. When a created being subjects itself to the slavery of evil and sees it as good, it is not only changed superficially as happens so often in our life, but is shaken up to its very depths. That is why honest men try quite naturally to protect the child from evil, and to surround it with goodness and love. Such men sense danger instinctively, and soon realize that their own strength is not enough. The child is living too deeply inside the mystery. With a piece of wood and a few rags in its hands, it can dream up a whole world of the imagination, a world beyond the world of its experience, a transcendental world.

The child lives, not here but somewhere beyond this world, so all real help, all true protection, must come to it from over there. This has led to the magnificent concept of "guardian angels" which, by way of St Paul's angelic teaching, have become part of the truth of Christ. If we want to understand this transcendental guardianship of children, not as "magical" event but as power always surrounding the child and given to its soul, then we must accept that God reveals himself directly to the child as the meaning and intensity of its life in the world, and its relationship to things. This is to postulate, only hypothetically of course, a specific kind of mysticism, different from any other form of experiencing God: a super-natural, existential mysticism that is really given by grace, but is never absent from the child's actual existence; a mysticism that penetrates all other aspects and states of the child's life—a funda-mental, inescapable element of that life. God is present to the child uninterruptedly, in a direct and non-verbalized relationship, as the background of its life and experience—in a way that does not bring God, as object of human thought, into the sphere of the sayable, but only enables the child to receive him unreflectively, perhaps as the "light of vision". The passage in the Gospel where Christ embraces a child is therefore, in our view, to be interpreted not merely historically or symbolically, but really and ontologically. Thus the grandeur and the dangers of child-life, and the transcen-dental protection which shines forth from it, are the three elements, in the light of which a Christian anthropology of childhood could be developed.[3] We must nevertheless remember that the three basic realities of childhood are only aspects of the one fundamental reality of all human life—the immediacy of the perceived nature of things and events.

The Woman: Tenderness

Our attempt to understand the woman and her life from the point of view of tenderness does not mean that we think this exhausts the mystery of womanhood; nor do we want to give women second place and put them back into the sphere of the sentimental, the pleasing and the basically trivial. The contrary is the case. Tender-ness is nothing weak or inferior. It is the height of feeling which protects the lovely things of the world, encounters them with re-spect and treats them with the dignity of restraint. The woman is directly immersed in the mystery of life. She knows about the frailty of life, and understands the often bewildering contexts of the world not so much through theories and concepts but through

3. G. Siewerth's *Metaphysik der Kindheit* (Einsiedeln, 1957) is inform-ative on the "anthropology of childhood".

the immediacy of life itself. She is entirely capable—recent investigations of intelligence potential shows this unambiguously—of holding her own with man in the intellectual and spiritual spheres. But her great gift is precisely her tenderness towards the vulnerable. And life is largely made up of them. One of the most significant insights of value philosophy consists in the realization that the highest value seems weak, threatened, unable to subsist, when brought into conjunction with lower values.

When life first appeared in the course of evolution it was extremely frail—produced by accident, prone to accidental destruction, continually at risk. The human spirit was no less weak when it first emerged from the animal world—searching, doubting, carrying man away from his comfortable earlier way of life. And the higher insights of this spirit (for example, that gentleness can be stronger than violence) seem feeble in their turn, unfitted for the world of every day. They are made to take back place and held to be immature. The man of silence goes unnoticed in a circle of quick talkers. The contemplation of beauty, costing nothing, seems pointless in a world of practical utilities. Hope, placed against other more tangible virtues, lacks strength, certainty and resolution. How little has man understood Christ's moral teaching—in essence the Sermon on the Mount—over the years. How easily his dreams shatter on hard reality. We do not see the significance of a man who lives his life according to the demands of love, is easy-tempered, friendly and self-less, lacks competitiveness, refrains from boasting, does not exaggerate his own powers, nor seek his own advantage, does not let himself be embittered, does not dwell on evil, rejoices in truth and not in injustice. The man who seeks to live his life according to the Being of all beings, in heaven, only seems eccentric to us. And finally—let us think about the powerlessness and absence of God in the world.

There is a continuous line from the first awakening of life to God who is its completion. And everywhere we see the same basic law at work: creation, growth in power, life evolving upwards, the breakthrough to reality—all these are simultaneously, and essentially, a process of the tender becoming more tender, the threatened becoming still more threatened, the endangered still more at risk. The Cross in the Christian sense, salvation in failure, is a cosmic law of ascent which found in Christ, the tenderest of all living things, its highest realization. It is woman's great dignity that she is completely taken over by this fundamental law of life, feels it often in her own body and soul, and has the gift of intuitive understanding of it. She is the being who can stand quietly, perhaps even wounded, under the cross of life, waiting for the resurrection. The woman as representative of life's ascent, which however culminates almost at once in crucifixion, is our subject matter here. We shall try to understand her essence from the point of view of tenderness, and tenderness only. She has many other qualities, all merging into each other, but these I shall leave to others more qualified than I to expound. We shall speak only about tenderness. In the depths of our experience of the being that is woman, we shall find, over and above the beauty, loveliness and dangers inherent in her, that quality of tenderness which is her last and most valuable gift to us.

Her own life is at risk, precisely because of her relationship to the tender and the fragile. But this necessarily puts her under God's protection, and she remains transcendentally protected as long as she is loyal to her obligation to tenderness. Revelation describes the relationship of the Absolute to Creation in a final image of a God who leads the whole world home as his bride to fulfilment. The woman has to feel God's special nearness inwardly, not so much as a fact but rather as an atmosphere—as God's special love for her. For—where else would she obtain her equally mysterious power to bring tenderness into a world given over to destruction, and through destruction entering into fulfilment.[4]

4. On the "anthropology of womanhood" I mention only one of many works: F. J. J. Buytendijk's *De Vrouw. Haar Natuur, verschijning en bestaan* (Amsterdam, 1952).

The Old: Light

What can an old person give us that belongs exclusively to him alone? His vitality has probably disappeared. He no longer possesses the strength to be creative. The dynamic of battle and conquest is no longer active in him. At first it seems as though little remains to him. If he clings to this littleness, his life becomes meaningless. Nevertheless there is a strength in the old that is different from the dynamic of creation and realization—the strength of wisdom attained through the experiences of a lifetime, and through the nearness of death.

On the one hand—an old man's hold on the future is increasingly tenuous. But for this very reason there rises up in his soul a wealth of past experience. What still holds him to life are thin threads and threadbare powers. Thus he is driven back to the ultimates that make up human life. And the essence of life, those mysterious strands which bind him to existence, is thereby revealed. The years have flown by. Did he dream his youth or had it been real? What he thought valuable—did it really have weight? He remembers decisions that never came to anything, beautiful things he never experienced in their fullness. His life was ultimately only a life of inner wastefulness, and the constant seeping away of his own self. All appearances, undertakings, all recreation, all life's skills and worldliness, all sense of endeavour and strength of action, were they not attempts to seem what he could not be in fact?[5] Were they not a flight before the fact of being what he was? He now begins to realize that his great troubles were not the result of what happened to him, but of what he was and is. Thus the pitiful and hateful aspects of his life enter into his consciousness and take a firm hold there. Of course all these aspects were already present in childhood, but there they were perhaps hidden by youthful hopefulness. Later came the feeling of growing maturity, and with it the confidence

5. On the anthropology of old age, see especially R. Guardini's short but remarkably thorough work: *Die Lebensalter* (Würzburg, 1967).

that everything was going well. But now he has arrived at the edge of existence, at the limits of life's powers, and there remain only fear and satiety. The feeling of being closed in on himself rises to the surface, and never again leaves him: I am this man and no other; never can I be anyone else. I am the man I have become from out of the innumerable possibilities of my life.

But on the other hand—this feeling of life drawing in, of the closeness of death, makes him clear-sighted in a curious, even rather frightening way. The question arises: If everything is ultimately going the way which I am inevitably moving, if all life is subject to death, if every Spring must sooner or later wither away, if every happy moment already has the smell of death in it, if the whole world is like this, what remains of human life at all? Perhaps there are moments when man sees himself lying there, motionless, stretched out, a corpse, while the world goes on around him. He sees his friends pursuing their own affairs; one of them makes preparations for his burial, and with kindly efficiency deals with the things he left unfinished in his life. But after a time his friends no longer know what to do about him. They remember him less and less often. Their memories of him grow weaker. And even those who still occasionally remember him grow fewer and fewer. If one thinks about all this, not with bitterness but in a mood of ultimate resignation, one may come to feel that one's life had been essentially a failure. There are few, really only very few, moments which were worth all the trouble. If eternal life exists, then we should like to take it with us into the endless Beyond. In this mood of resignation at our own failure, we remember certain magical moments from out of the present conflict—some instances of loneliness endured, of true selflessness; a few moments keeping company with a dear friend; some good deeds wrested from our own heart; certain insights which we suddenly notice we cannot exactly "prove"; then too, suffering endured; faithfulness perhaps to the point of despair; the "nevertheless" of hope in the midst of failure; a helping hand, a kind glance, first love and so on. These we want to take with us into eternal life—the things that happened, so to speak, incidentally in our life.

In this way man acquires wisdom through ultimate renunciation. In so doing, and in the measure in which he thinks about all this in the final moments of honesty given to all whose life draws to a close, he is given the power and light of patience for his broken life. The wise man no longer possesses knowledge but is filled with an increasing measure of resignation, a delicate love for what is done without counting the cost, a tenderness for what is squandered away. With a quiet smile he observes how life passes by, the detours it makes, the way it tarries here and there, the pleasure it takes in flowering over-abundantly, the opportunities it gives to the superfluous and apparently foolish, how curiously it seems to contradict all that is utilitarian and carefully ordered; and how it is precisely this that constitutes its most valuable element. Thus man waits— quietly and with fresh knowledge. He watches life as it waits idly, winding itself into knots, becomes hesitant, uncertain and undecided, till it frees itself again and finds its right direction. He comes to terms with what is incomplete, puts up with faults, protects the unsuccessful and surrounds them with that mysterious love which is not only compassion but also a sense of hidden solidarity in life. The old are the guardians of one of the most precious and simplest mysteries of the world, and are themselves protested by it—God's patience with creation.[6]

We have tried, by means of a brief analysis of three forms of human existence—that of the child, the woman and the old—to penetrate into the mysterious dimension of life that is referred to as "protected". In so doing we have discovered a law of being which can be changed into a definition of human life: Man is the being who, in guarding what is tender and threatened, is himself protected by it and is thereby shown God's power. This delicate, fragile insight—which must be protected in its turn—is shown in

6. See R. Guardini, *Glaubenserkenntnis* (Freiburg i.Br., 1949), especially the section entitled "Gottes Geduld", pp. 21 ff).

the Bible by the story of Tobit (Tobias). It is a legendary tale well known to us all, but we shall nevertheless relate it briefly here.

The story of Tobit begins with an account of two people simultaneously unhappy before the face of God. On the one hand there is the story of an old and devout man, who has endured much suffering—the aged Tobit. He was almost the only one still living in his own country, Israel, who faithfully observed God's law. He lived according to the spirit of the God who loves men and had compassion for them, and he carefully looked after the poorest of his oppressed and frightened people. He was "carried away captive to Nineveh"—with his wife and son. There he remained doing good works, took care of the abandoned and buried the dead. He carried on in this way, despite many blows of fate. But at the end he could go on no longer: poor, blind, forsaken by all, he turned to God and implored him to take him out of this world, where he no longer possessed hope (Tob. 1. 3–3. 6).

On the other hand there is the story of a young, unhappy woman. At roughly the same time Sarah in Media decided to hang herself in her upper chamber. She had already been given to seven husbands, but all seven died before they could consummate the marriage. Thus she became the subject of mockery and insult, and could no longer endure it. But she did not want to grieve her father, so instead of hanging herself she prayed to God with outstretched arms before her window, asking him to take away her life (Tob. 3. 7–15). Thus two people are breaking under their sufferings. An old man and a young woman find themselves in their prayers at the edge of despair. But there appears to them from out of the sphere of the transcendent the figure of their protector, the angel, the messenger of God to the world, to set them free (Tob. 3. 16–17). Their liberation is effected by young Tobias, the son of Tobit, who is still partly a child, but already at the onset of manhood. He is protected by the angel.

This son is sent on a dangerous journey to fetch a considerable sum of money from a certain Gabael in Media for his father. With good advice and great trepidation his parents bid farewell to Tobias, as he gets ready for the journey in the company of the angel.[7] The angel guides Tobias on his journey and knows how to protect him— he aids him in danger, teaches him the use of various remedies (against the blindness of his father and against evil demons), prepares him for the meeting with his beautiful, honourable and gracious cousin Sarah, and reminds him of the laws of kinship and inheritance in regard to her, which the young man Tobias does not find difficult to fulfil, in view of Sarah's charms. Both young people, obeying the instructions of the angel, survive the dangerous wedding night, to the great surprise of the young woman's parents. The marriage feast lasts fourteen days. During this time the angel fetches the money from Gabael who accepts an invitation to appear at the wedding feast in person. But in the meantime Tobias' parents have become very anxious. The days the journey was expected to take have passed, and still their son has not returned. The wife of old Tobias goes out every day, in order to watch the road. Young Tobias, on his side, is restless and urges a return. So the great procession sets out for home (Tob. 4. 1–10. 13).

Tobias and the angel hurry on in advance and the joy of reunion knows no bounds, especially as the angel's medicament enables old Tobias really to see his son again. The old man hastens to meet his daughter-in-law and brings her to the house. The day turns into a feast day for all the Jews in Nineveh. But for the angel it is time to take farewell. He reveals his real nature as God's angel, messenger and protector, gives them advice and suggestions for the future, reveals God's mysterious plans and finally "ascends". "Then they stood up; but they saw him no more. So they confessed the great and wonderful works of God, and acknowledged that the angel of the Lord had appeared to them" (Tob. 11. 1–12. 21). The days of old Tobit and his wife end in quiet happiness. The old man Tobit dies during a vision of Israel's return from captivity, the conversion

7. R. M. Rilke, *Duino Elegies* (2nd Elegy, verses 4–5).

of all the peoples on the earth and the coming of God's kingdom in the eternal Jerusalem. After young Tobias had buried his parents in Nineveh, he returns with all his goods and possessions to Media to his parents-in-law, whom he surrounds with respectful attention in their old age. The time passes happily. The parents-in-law also die, Tobias inherits their property and lives with his wife Sarah and his children to the age of 127. He lives to see the first signs of the coming of God's kingdom proclaimed by his father (Tob. 13. 1–14. 15). Thus ends the story about threats and good fortune, danger and protection, pious living and obedient death, human loyalty and the visit of the angel, earthly destiny and divine goodness.

It is a story, perhaps only a legend, told with great tenderness; and contained within it is the revelation of human reality in its ultimate aspect of needing and giving protection. Yet human life does not return to idyll in the story. The tremendous reality of God is not minimized. Basically the story as it is literally told is not all that important. The real revelation is contained in the attitude to life that is shown, and the way in which the story is related. Everything is told positively, from the point of view of life, belief in life, taste for happiness, enthusiasm for being, a feeling of being alive that is immeasurably richer and more renewing than logic, a recognition of the "fullness" that we can discover in every growing spirit, especially in times of change and danger.[8] It is the attitude of faith in providence.

The real depths, the so to say basic structure of life, is shown in the salvational aspect of the world by two concepts, which can on their side be referred back to the fundamental experience of being protected—blessing and good fortune. A mysterious quality belongs to the whole of being—that of being blessed.

8. See J. Daniélou, "Gottes Wiederentdeckung" (*Wort und Wahrheit*, vol. 17, Aug/Sept. 1962, Nos. 8/9, pp. 517 f).

Being Blessed

The Bible describes the creation of the world as a flood of divine goodwill, bearing the world towards an everlasting fulfilment of infinite beatitude—despite all evidence to the contrary in the sphere of the visible, despite sin and corruption, despite rebellion and hardening of heart. This mysterious power is at work from the very beginning. The whole human race is blessed from its origin, and in the human race and on its behalf, the entire world is blessed also. This blessing is clearly shown in a whole series of devout men, from whom it shines out into the rest of creation. God's blessing, however, is more and more concentrated as time goes on in an insignificant peoples; and among these peoples is a small remnant of especially faithful and holy men. From out of the whole world, from all humanity, from among the specially blessed, and the specially receptive, there emerges in a long-drawn-out process a single being in whom the blessing of God takes on pure human form, Jesus Christ. His life thus consists in taking everything blessed into himself and leading it safely into a sphere where it can live and grow for all eternity. Here a new world is born that is all blessing. Here man himself appears in his indestructible reality, and real life begins in eternal happiness. It is this kind of summary of salvation history that shows clearly the "infallibility" with which God leads the world and the human race towards happiness. No created power can oppose this movement; no one can prevent its ultimate flowering. In this sense the pre-determinism of the world, its predestination, is nothing other than the infallibility of a God whose benevolence, like all true love, does not fail and does not let itself be driven away, but includes everything, even rejection, in a still greater love. The attitude of joy in living comes out of our life as its existential answer.

Bliss

This is the conscious dependence on God's goodness changed into a basic attitude of joy in everyday life. It often comes out of an oppressed heart, struggling against the despair of the world, against poverty, tears, mourning, against oppression, injustice, lack of fulfilment. In this view all the darker aspects of revelation that are an indubitable part of it—the moments of destruction, of threats, of suffering and darkness—are in no sense signs of God's punishment. God has committed himself absolutely, and from the beginning of creation He has predestined the world for His blessing in ever richer measure. There is no going back on his "once and for all". His blessing, and with it the happiness it promises, grows and develops in the world, and nothing can stop it.

But to be really happy, to welcome the living blessing of God in our heart, our life must free itself, must open outwards, must break through the layers and deposits of selfishness, must become totally receptive. The paradox is this: The love of God, which is pure love and nothing else, can appear to us in the dark garb of punishment, although in essence it excludes every aspect of it. Human love can seem very similar. It is only when we experience the natural tie, the clarity and light that come to us as a result of the attraction exercised by a loved friend, that we begin to suffer under our love. It acts like fire in our soul, so that everything that is not worthy of it burns up in it. In me who am linked to another human being in a oneness of love, there can exist only what is beautiful, constructive, joy-bearing and enriching. It is not punishment to be made truly worthy of such love, but the longing of the human heart. Suffering, death, purgatory, judgment, punishment and other dark theological concepts have no need for demythologization, since revelation has already demythologized these concepts in the radical, unequalled statement that God's being is love and nothing other than love.

In the light of the above there can be no further doubt that an atmosphere of joy and happiness are signs of holiness' presence in human life. Christian holiness in our world is built upon fidelity to joy and happiness—often amidst suffering neither recognized nor suspected by others, and inner exhaustion. But all this takes place under God's eye—under the protection of him who embraces all life with unceasing tenderness, especially those areas where it is most seriously threatened and at risk.

7. Happy Man

IF we want to understand human life in its most fundamental aspect, then we must examine the concept of happiness. The existence of happiness cannot be denied. We have all experienced those moments of light that enabled our life to be seen in its inner reality. From out of the muddle of daily existence there suddenly emerges an ultimate meaning—happiness—which sets up in us a feeling of holy awe. This then is what my life is like in its depths—so light, so clear, so fulfilling and so "different". We are confronted by a life that is truly our own, made of the same stuff as we ourselves, embracing our total destiny. And yet at the same time it is no longer our life but something given us, something indescribable.

Our life is taken over by a curious mood—not of joy nor of sadness; nothing high nor deep. It does not belong into the world of our normal feelings and moods. It is pure existence, deeply rooted and wide open—it is happiness. The whole of life becomes transparent, visible from within; feels itself related to everything else and yet remains itself, does not dissolve. To experience infinity when finite —that is happiness. What is learnt and experienced at such times can scarcely be analysed. It exists totally within itself and cannot be referred back to anything else. Although the experience itself cannot be described, it remains irrefutable for all who have known such moments either in their own lives, or in the life of those they love. If we could speak of our bliss, then we should have discovered the language with which to speak of heaven. But one thing we can attempt—and that is the subject of the intellectual efforts we shall be making in this chapter—to name and to try to understand the basic conditions in which happiness can grow. There are eight of these.

First: Poverty

Poverty can be called the first precondition for happiness because in poverty—in so far as it is not merely material privation but an existential attitude to life—man makes the fundamental decision not to equate himself, his true self, with his mere presence. I "am" more than all that I "have". In this decision he breaks through to freedom. He does not let anything constrict his life, he allows no earthly possessions to bar his way into the unknown. He is more than all that he has achieved in life, all that he has realized, known and come to love. He feels a sense of existential freedom.

No one can take my real self away from me. I can go to meet the greater reality fresh and carefree, without letting myself be tied by anything whatsoever. I can let myself be at the service of everything, can stay quietly with the beauty of the world, but can also be available to men in their cares and sorrows. Essentially spiritual poverty is the openness of a loving heart that does not mind whether it is greatly successful, whether the superficial things of life elude it. The soul begins to listen and does not obtrude itself. It rises above the power of the routine and commonplace. It lets itself be taken beyond itself, is open to an ever-new present. The first instinctive move of one who has been interiorly set free is an unassuming benevolence towards things, people and events, and not the desire to possess.

This is a creative "being together" which can continue to exist even when it is not returned, when it is misunderstood or rejected. Such inner liberation leads to that movement towards inwardness out of which grows, in its turn, the ability of vision. Man wants things for their own sake and not in order to make use of them. He can live in the other world; he knows how to be still and open. He does not possess the world. But the world gives itself to him in a profounder way than ever happened when he had possessions. Thus he lives a "liberated life", capable of vision, and filled with knowledge. People open their most secret selves to such a person, for they know that they will not be used or made use of, will not be manipulated, not find themselves in alien circumstances, but will be received as individuals, joyful and needy. A new world grows round such a person—nature in an attitude of surrender, a world of individuals, secure and accepted. "Blessed are the poor in spirit, for theirs is the kingdom of heaven" (Mt. 5. 3).[1]

Second: Mourning

The attitude of letting go of self, called "poverty in spirit" enables man really to live with the world. This entails not only a special quality of receptiveness and sympathy, but in addition the ability to share the life of strangers. Such a man feels especially drawn to the oppressed and humble—to people therefore, who are at the mercy of their misfortunes. Without premeditation, and often with shyness, he lays himself open to the pain of others. He grows inwardly silent in the face of their suffering, and takes their human frailty upon himself. Those who take part in his "banquet" are the poor, the blind, the maimed, the lame (Luke 14. 12–14). A curious unrest seizes hold of him. He feels he wants to break away from his normal life, and have "nowhere to lay his head" (Mt. 8. 20), so that he will be all the more ready to give of himself to all who are oppressed. It is blessedness for him no longer to belong to himself, and to share the danger of others.

A man who is moved like this by the sufferings of others does not go to his suffering brothers in the attitude of teacher, or helper, from outside, with feelings of sad sympathy. No he takes their very sufferings upon himself. This is more than simply brotherly readiness to help, or social welfare. These are present also, and indeed must be, if the helper wants to prove his willingness to help. But the over-all attitude goes deeper. It lies in the expression, the "more" of love, that makes us willing to let our own life be darkened by the darkness of another's pain.

1. See J. B. Metz, *Armut im Geiste* (Munich, 1962).

To undergo another's inescapable destiny, to endure for long periods the wretchedness of another's life, to share the humiliation of a broken existence, not out of sentimentality or mere emotion but from an attitude to life that has become second nature—this is the mourning that in its darkness surrounds everyone who loves self-lessly in a cold world threatened by suffering and death. The sadness of such mourning can exhaust a man, can make his life hollow and empty. Man becomes insecure, frightened and tired. But he constantly pulls himself together and gives himself anew, even if his giving is no longer understood. Such a man has delivered himself over to the mourning of the world, and has thereby acquired a deep understanding of human life.

By slow degrees, in a gradual process of faithfulness and endurance, there is formed in such people a deep central core that transcends the accident of mood, of superficial proofs and external appearances. There, in that central core, a new dimension of life appears consolation, the bliss of "no longer belonging to oneself", of being "taken out of oneself", of inner self-surrender. Such people live the essence of their life already in a mysterious "beyond", from where strength continually flows towards them. They live in resignation, free from false appearances and self-pity. Somehow they have already departed from this world. We see only the shadow of their greatness in our own consoled life. "Blessed are those who mourn, for they shall be comforted" (Mt. 5. 4).[2]

Third: Mildness

The joyful readiness to let go of self (spiritual poverty) changes and develops into a determination to open oneself to the suffering of the world (mourning). Thus man develops a new quality of being, an in-built reverence for life. This deeply-rooted, firmly-based attitude

2. See R. Guardini, *Der Herr* (Würzburg, 1951, pp. 81 f, 88 f, 103; Eng. trans.: *The Lord*).

of reverence, amidst all the contradiction and bewilderments of the world, is what we call the courage of mildness or gentleness. It is not the virtue of the weak but of the inwardly strong, who do not feel the need for revenge, for repaying "like with like".

But this is only the negative aspect of mildness. The positive element consists in a feeling of sympathy for all created beings, especially those who are ill-disposed towards us. Of course mildness also expresses itself in other forms—in restraint, in non-coercion in the absence of presumption, in a stillness of gaze and recognition, in delicacy of speech and sensibility of relationships. But where it proves itself greatest, where it extends to the very edge of human capability and shows itself in its pure state, is in the "love of one's enemy". This does not mean a cowardly putting up with what is wrong and unjust, or a failure to work for truth and justice. Nor does it prevent man from defending precious, lovable and living things from attacks by evil. Thus it is not a blurring of the edges or explaining away of contradictions.

"Loving one's enemy" is nothing artificial, but simply the age-old movement of a loving heart: "For me you are no enemy—not in your innermost heart. However many contradictions and differences exist between us, and even if I should have to defend myself against the injustice that you want to do to me, there is no enmity between us. I do not want to be victorious over you, or humiliate you, or hurt you in any way. I do not even want to assert myself against you. I do not hate you. Indeed I feel that you are especially in need of my love because so many other things separate us." Without such fundamental sympathy and loving attraction for the person of the enemy, man cannot acquire that quiet recollection which is a precondition for happiness. His soul will be poisoned by hateful thoughts feelings and ideas of rejection and revenge, and thus will not be truly itself. His mind will not be able to free itself of these things but will be immersed in a negative self-determination, and become the slave of the person it hates, indeed the slave of the hatred it directs against him. This is the worst state of loss into which man can throw himself. And as long as he remains in this condition, he cannot calmly possess anything, cannot freely enjoy anything, cannot completely give himself to beauty, truth or fulfilling love. He can no longer be close to the earth, can no longer "inherit" it.

The love of one's enemy, on the other hand, is the highest expression of human freedom. It reveals the superiority of the human mind, its ruling greatness. The encounter with such people is the greatest benefit that we can know. Their office among us is simply not to hate. Their power over men's minds is great because it is entirely inward—total attraction and total goodness. Such people can truly become "shepherds of souls", indeed "shepherds of life". Other men instinctively seek refuge with them. All being opens itself out to them, calmly and quietly. Such people will never hurt us: "Blessed are the meek, for they shall inherit the earth" (Mt. 5. 5).[3]

Fourth: Longing

Once a person is free of self, open to the world and prepared to love everything and everyone, the "real" world begins to grow in and around him, the sense of being completely at home. Everything in life arranges itself in a fixed order. The soul of such a man becomes a happy dwelling place for him. Within it, he has true freedom of manoeuvre. He can be all truth, and need not be ashamed of it or try to dissemble. He can be all goodness, and will not be used or robbed. He can be completely, uniquely himself, in a new oneness of life, without being misunderstood, and without having to experience the destruction of his inner oneness. He can reveal his inner richness; he can be "beautiful" without awakening envy or greed, without making himself a laughing stock. In a word—he can be true, good, unique and beautiful, and find his fulfilment thereby.

3. Cf. my *In Time of Temptation* (London, 1968).

We are referring here to that state of being at peace with the world
that has been incomparably described in Isaiah:

> The wolf shall dwell with the lamb,
>   and the leopard shall lie down with the kid,
> and the calf and the lion and the fatling together,
>   and a little child shall lead them,
> the cow and the bear shall feed;
>   their young shall lie down together,
>   and the lion shall eat straw like the ox.
> The suckling child shall play over the hole of the asp,
>   and the weaned child shall put his hand on the adder's den.
> They shall not hurt or destroy
>   in all my holy mountain;
> for the earth shall be full of the
>   knowledge of the Lord
> as the waters cover the sea.
>
> (Is. 11. 6–9)

The truth of these lines lies as much in the description of peace, of
abundance, of beauty and clarity, as in the impossibility of the situation, the irreconcilable and contradictory images. The "right
order of things", the being at peace with the world, is thus the most
beautiful, but also the unattainable, object of our longing.

Justice (*sedek*) is not yet a reality. It is given us only exception-
ally. It is sometimes concentrated in unusually self-less, open and
gentle people, or better still, in groups of people who long for it.
Their very longing carries fulfilment within itself in the form of
promise.

There exists at the same time an undercurrent in the history of the
human race—those who long, who have nothing, who know that
they are hopelessly poor, hungry and needy, day in day out, in
everything they do. Mostly they are "little people", who nevertheless never cease to long for ultimate fulfilment. And although they
have been longing for so long, although they have given up so much,

have given so much of their heart's blood and have always, all the time, been disappointed, deceived and lied to, they cannot agree to give up hope. Why? Here we have the inner evidence of longing itself, the presence of fulfilment, the existence of the goal of their longing as a constituent element of their desire. It is the inner evidence of the "attainability of the unattainable"—the direct understanding of the words "Blessed are those who hunger and thirst for righteousness, for they shall be satisfied" (Mt. 5. 6).[4]

Fifth: Mercy

A person who is filled with longing, and impelled by an unsatisfied desire for greatness, feels himself at one with those who are also unfulfilled, with sufferers. This is not due to condescension, but to a fundamental relationship with those who are undergoing the same human necessity. There is, so to speak, a secret society of all who are truly suffering, an association of people without masks—who hunger, mourn, thirst, who are harassed and persecuted. But not of those who make a virtue of poverty, wretchedness and hunger, who are piously resigned to their fate, who like to see themselves at its mercy, who make a display of themselves, who cleverly know how to fill the emptiness of their lives, who skilfully interpret their sickness as health, who explain their hunger as satiety. Nor of those who go about in masks, behind which they hide their disfigured, eaten up faces. No one can find happiness in masks.

The urge for happiness comes upon us when we are hungry, and it demands nourishment. The thirst in us asks for drink. Naked life is cold and wants to be clothed. Prisoners dream of freedom. The sick man hopes for health; and he who has lost himself seeks the way home. The ignorant feel themselves hemmed in and long for light. Doubters ask their friends for advice. The sad are in search of consolation. Injustice cries out for justice. He who has handed out

4. See Ernst Bloch, *Das Prinzip Hoffnung* (Frankfurt a.M., 1959), vols. 1–2.

insults wants forgiveness. And all the living—and even the dead
—wait for the loving nearness of friendship.

Thus how can a man who has never yet been hungry, sick, unknown, empty, abandoned and hopelessly alone—how can such a
one really understand human wretchedness? Can he take it upon
himself and into his innermost being? Probably not. Perhaps he will
approach another's misery very solemnly and with great kindness
will want to take it upon himself and bear it in the other's place. But
he is not able to do this. Not in the last resort. Not where suffering
ceases to have meaning. No one can take my pain from me, my sin,
my loss. These things are not objects of barter. No one can take
from me my birth or my death, and no one can take my fallenness
away from me. But someone who has himself experienced the sense-
lessness of suffering can sit beside me, when I am sad and feel lost—
not saying a word. I shall feel that he is my friend, who cannot perhaps do anything for me except be sad with me. Thus in my mourning I shall no longer be alone. Perhaps this will console me. This
sitting beside me will seem meaningless unless he is my friend.
There can be no other explanation for it. He cannot voice his sympathy differently. He too has no answers, but he is wearing no mask.
The God of salvation must come down into this society of the
maskless, if he wants to live our pain, if he wants to be our friend,
the friend of the despairing little ones. But that he seats himself
beside us, hollowed out, empty, hungry, dedicated to death, even
God-abandoned, will only be seen by those who have the courage
to count themselves among the number of the lost and are themselves capable of sitting beside all the others who are lost, as their
friend. Such merciful ones will be able to see God's mercy. The
others will not even notice the insignificant little man with the
divine longing. "Blessed are the merciful, for they shall obtain
mercy" (Mt. 5. 7).[5]

5. See my *Der Anwesende Gott* (Olten, 1969, the section entitled *Das
Erbarmen*, pp. 69 ff).

Sixth: Purity

Up to this point we have tried to analyse the inner reality of human happiness by concentrating on the essence of human joy, the element of "not belonging to oneself", and its increasingly wide implications. The man who is poor in spirit approaches things, events and people with an open mind. He lets human life, even including deepest mourning, take complete possession of him. He excludes no one from participation in his sympathy, and uses gentleness even against his enemy. There is a longing in him that carries him out and beyond the smallnesses of life to a marvellous promise of a real world. He wants his friends, the oppressed and fearful, somehow to share in the happiness of this blissful transformation, and thus he tries to assuage their pain through his selfless presence. We can see how this must lead to a new quality of life, of being oneself through letting go of self.

Something clean, unspoilt, unselfconscious is present here— the purity of life, being as transparency. By and by everything pertaining to fear, narrowness and hypocrisy (the displacement of reality) disappears from such a life, and a lively joy becomes his natural state. Joy and peace now reign in him, generosity, openheartedness, tolerance and simple brotherliness begin to grow. Everything around him becomes quiet and clear. Life itself grows confiding. It is a power full of mystery. It is not a power that can break him now. It is not magnificence like that of gigantic mountains or stormy seas. It is the power of clarity, of transparency, the clear light of a bright day or of a person in complete possession of himself. It is the power of beauty, of life grown into oneness, that wants nothing of us, does not urge itself upon us, gives us everything it has and thus is blessed.

Nevertheless the witness of a pure being moves us more than all the power in the world. What we see here is instinctive happiness living for others—clear undivided being. And when such a being gives itself to us, we are overwhelmed, the giving is so total and so unconditional. We are tempted to cry, "No, you cannot do this. I am not worthy of your giving." And yet it happens as a simple matter of course, like a flower or a vase or a tree whose outline is ours while its real self remains pure and untouched. Such people are truth for us. To meet them is one of the greatest graces of our life. Their openness and self-surrender are proof that somehow they look through us into an eternity, into absolute Being, which we cannot see. They already look on God, and are with him amidst all the wretchedness of the world. "Blessed are the pure in heart, for they shall see God" (Mt. 5. 8).[6]

Seventh: Foundations

Such people have something curiously creative about them. They make "foundations". They do holy works of grace in our world. Their principal—and unassuming—work is peace. They do not discover new aspects of being, they do not create new thought or trends. They are concerned with what is already there, and with arranging it in proper order. It is a humble task that most will forget or claim later for themselves. And it requires restraint. Those who establish peace stay unremarked. They are dealing with death-bringing emotions and setting them at rest; they let feelings crash against each other and unload themselves; they look for ways and means and ways out, and carry on like this for a long time, if it proves to be necessary.

Only the man who is firmly rooted in truth can establish peace, without insult and compromise. Truth must be born for everyone out of contradiction. The "founder" is simply there, and when the birth has taken place, he withdraws. But his work continues to glow as though of itself, and all think, "I have done this." This is one of the most difficult works of selfless love. Man must give of himself, he must enter into the destruction of the other, must be totally with

6. See also Gregory of Nyssa's *Kommentar zum Hohe Lied* (PG 44, 756–1120). German: *Der versiegelte Quell* (Einsiedeln, 1954).

him. But at the same time he must preserve an inner purity, must be firmly rooted, modest and calm. To bring peace to a broken soul— that can only be done by someone who has himself either found inner peace already, or whose life is spent in the search for peace. And peace is only achieved for a little time. Then the harmony built up with such effort threatens to break apart again. Thus when peace shines out from a man, God himself seems to be at work, to be present among us.

The "god of love and peace" (2 Cor. 13. 11) shines through him. "For in him [Christ] all the fullness of God was pleased to dwell, and through him to reconcile to himself all things, whether on earth or in heaven, making peace by the blood of his cross" (Col. 1. 20). All likeness to Christ in our world, all resemblance to God's son, who is "our peace" (Eph. 2. 14) is concentrated on the man who brings peace. God's sons are truly in the world, and their life is proof of the existence and the person of Christ. Even meeting with them can give one a distant feeling of the presence of Christ himself, and of the "blood of his cross". "Blessed are the peacemakers, for they shall be called sons of God" (Mt. 5. 9).[7]

Eighth: Suffering

The figure of a happy man came very close to us just now, to enable us to be overwhelmed by its presence. But at the same time we must be aware how great the danger is for such a person, how helplessly he is delivered over to human suffering. There is a pain of happiness, a cross of happiness. For no greater suffering exists than to bear happiness within oneself and at the same time to share the human sense of loss, to feel happiness and loss, both at once. These are not externally imposed on the happy man, but are given him to complete his happiness. For his happiness consists in the fact that he shares the lot of the lost, and faithfully participates in their destiny, in

7. See K. Rahner, *Einübung priestlicher Existenz* (Freiburg i. Br., 1970; pp. 237 ff).

order to establish justice in the world. The real world will become a place where all shall be at home, where they can live at peace with one another, as has earlier been shown in the eschatological vision of Isaiah:

> The wolf shall dwell with the lamb
> and the leopard shall lie down with the kid,
> and the calf and the lion and the fatling together,
> and a little child shall lead them.

That is the situation of the good man. It is not brought about by magic, but by human hands; it is suffered in a human soul, borne with human fidelity. Thus the good man comes close to us in friendship. Yet his life is strange to us, removed from ours into a sphere of suffering only guessed at by us, but never experienced in its depths.

When theology wants to understand, at least in outline, the life of Christ, she links two basic principles very close together. She says that Christ was a man who lived totally in the "vision beatifico" (beatific vision) of God, and yet at the same time had committed the act of human daring that we call "descensus ad inferos" (descent into hell). In Christ it was the same "I" that rejoiced in the bliss of God's nearness, and could also say, "My soul is very sorrowful, even to death" (Mt. 26. 38). It was these two polarized experiences that so enlarged Christ's soul that it could contain within itself the whole of creation, "the breadth and length and height and depth" (Eph. 3. 18). Thus he became the fulfilment of all that is, the prince of a new kingdom of the world. "Blessed are those who are persecuted for righteousness' sake, for theirs is the kingdom of heaven" (Mt. 15. 10). To endure this, to be completely open to the mystery yet rooted in the depths to lost humanity—this too means happiness.[8]

We have made an honest attempt to come to an understanding of human happiness. Not those superficial wishes or desires that relate only to the appearance of things, but that deep awareness of human

8. See H. Vorgrimler, "Christ's Descent into Hell: Is it important"? *Concilium*, vol. I, January 1966; pp. 75 ff).

life fulfilled, that we have so often betrayed but could never quite forget. This is man—the figure of the happy man who emerges from out of such deep human awareness fully coincides with Christ's description in the Beatitudes of the essence of happiness. The Beatitudes are often depicted as something totally new, contradictory and paradoxical, that is to say "divine". But whoever speaks like this not only lacks thought but shows that he knows little about the depths to be found in human life. There is nothing new or startling in the beatitudes. Everything in them is thoroughly human and corresponds right down to the tiniest detail to the basic longing of life. We must not draw a caricature of humanity in order to underline the astonishing greatness of Christ's message. Human life is great enough already and infinitely transcends man himself. If we think truthfully about ourselves, we come to know Christ. It is not surprising that man as such can think, feel and long like this. What is surprising is that one man really succeeded in uniting and realizing all these longings and awarenesses in himself; that there was a man among us in whom all this suddenly fell into place. This was the overwhelming new insight of the Fathers. What is new in Christ is Christ himself. He did not bring new revelations but continually fulfilled it. He is the Amen of our life.[9]

Thus we come to a wider definition of Christian anthropology by summarizing the ideas discussed above: Man is the being that can find its way to happiness through poverty, mourning, gentleness, longing, mercy, purity, peacefulness and suffering, and obtain everlasting fulfilment of the powers that are deeply rooted in his being.

It is not possible fully to work out the anthropological ideas contained in this short statement. That is a task for a broadly based, radically Christian anthropology. Here it is sufficient for us to have attempted a first step into a still unchartered sea, to have opened up new dimensions and expressed new possibilities.

9. Ireneus of Lyon, *Adversus Haereses* IV, 12; 3 (PG 7. 1005/B); IV, 34; 1 (PG 7 1083/C).

It must be possible—if we believe Christ's reality to be the fulfilment of our humanity and if we insert this belief with intellectual strictness into our philosophy—to create a picture of man based on the Sermon on the Mount, the "fundamental anthropology of Christ". In that Sermon Christ really told us how he saw man. It is hard to understand why Christian anthropology has more or less failed in this field, lacking the courage to integrate the ideas proceeding from the Sermon on the Mount into its philosophy.

In this sense we can and must admit that for Christian anthropology man still remains—as described a little sensationally but basically correctly in the title of Alexis Carrel's book *Das unbekannte Wesen* (*The Unknown Being*). And he will remain so for as long as he does not radically align himself with Christ.

There is a pathological condition called "amnesia". It appeared quite often in connection with the war. A man lives, does this and that, but has forgotten who he is. His life thus lacks centre and unity. Something similar, but in monstrous proportions, has happened to the Christian image. The Christian seems to be a man who has forgotten his name, for his name is contained in the name of Christ himself. One cannot forget the name of Christ and remain true to one's own name, one's own path and meaning in life, as man and as Christian. The time has come for Christian anthropology to base itself on the totality of Christian experience in the Pauline sense: "All are yours; and you are Christ's" (1 Cor. 3. 23–24).[10]

10. H. de Lubac, *Essay on the Church.*

8. Seeking Man

ONE of the most important insights of modern anthropology, in which the Danish philosopher and theologian, Sören Kierkegaard, has most lastingly influenced our thinking, is the teaching about the different "stages" of human existence. We shall not be expounding his ideas here. We shall be dealing with the basic recognition that human life in its real sense is not something "given". It must be won by personal decision.

There are certain basic decisions in human life that are essential to the person. As such they represent the innermost aspects of human life. Man is continually searching for his own reality. Human life in its fullness is graded according to these decisions and the levels of existence that correspond to them. But there is no automatic path from one level to the next. Instead life must first be lived fully on one particular level. Man experiences the fullness, but also the dangers, of this one level of life. Slowly he comes to know his "dwelling place" as dubious and dangerous. A crisis of existence develops. And so he begins to feel more and more urgently the need to escape. He sees increasingly clearly that his whole being is more than can be realized by him in this given situation. After numerous experiences of longing, he reaches a situation where more daring attempts are required of him. The value of previous stages is not called into question or denied; but they are no longer sufficient for fulfilment. And so human life goes forward and upward into an ever-growing reality which, however, is not deducible from the previous situation. Human life grows by throwing itself in the unknown.[1]

Let us try to complete this insight by projecting it into our own

1. See R. Guardini, *Die Lebensalter* (Würzburg, 1967).

life. What are the boundaries that we have already crossed and the risks that we believe still await us? What decisions do we have to make, what destiny must we take upon ourselves?

Life in Security

Already at the beginning of this book we showed how threatened and at risk human life was. Thus it is always looking for protection and security—for home, warmth, friendship and love; and most of all for inner confirmation. What it finds it savours with all the immediacy of a living being. It feels fulfilled, enriched—or again empty and poor. But it is "feeling". What gives it security is not so much the things it has found out as the experience of its search. It is wonderful to be a seeker, to be able to choose one's fulfilment, to stay or go on according to one's inner urge. A curious feeling of displacement characterizes life at this level. Man floats over impressions and gathers from them only their sweetest elements. This fills him for the moment with deep emotion. But as soon as he has left behind the things he has half exhausted, he is filled with boredom and must seek for new experiences.

Slowly a deep-seated impatience takes hold of him, an inability to remain any longer in the same place. The hunt for new experience begins. But it is no longer a positive seeking, only a flight from inner emptiness. Such a man is at the mercy of the ephemeral; he only looks for fleeting pleasures and clings to the fickle current of the wind. Decisions are postponed, firm commitments avoided. The world itself loses its reality, becomes the plaything of vacillating emotions. Perhaps life is beautiful, but behind it lies the beginning of despair.

One starts to doubt the beauty of things. They are so quickly exhausted, and then immediately thrown away. Nothing is ultimately binding, nothing is final, nothing upheld, protected, borne aloft or cherished by man. Perhaps he throws himself with exaggerated energy into his work. He discards the values in which he believed his soul would find fulfilment. Such a man exercises a curious fascination. He is a firework of experiences, lit before the astounded eyes of the world. The rest of us imagine him to possess a mysterious richness of soul. We are drawn under his spell, try to capture him or find security in him. But suddenly we notice that behind his beautiful mask there is no longer a man.

In his *"Notebooks of Malte Laurids Brigge"* Rilke symbolically describes the despair of a man who lives behind masks. This is one of the most impressive descriptions of the last stage of existence that we are considering here. Rilke describes the experience of a child which, in the large corner room on an uninhabited floor of the magnificent house, discovers costumes, cloaks, materials and masks and disguises himself. It is a story symbolizing life, and told with inimitable sympathy and delicacy:

". . . I was still laughing as I disguised myself, and I completely forgot what I had intended to represent. But no matter; it was a novel and exciting experience to defer the decision until I should be standing before the mirror. The face I fastened on had an odour that made it feel singularly cavernous; it fitted closely to my own face, but I was able to see through it quite comfortably. Then, when the mask was on, I selected various kinds of scarves, which I bound about my head like a turban, in such a way that the edge of the mask, which reached downwards into an immense yellow cloak, was also almost entirely hidden on top and at the sides. At length, when I had exhausted my powers of invention, I considered myself sufficiently disguised. To complete the outfit I seized a large staff, which I held at my side, as far out as my arm could reach; and in this fashion, not without difficulty, but, as it seemed to me, full of dignity, I dragged myself along towards the mirror in the spare bedroom.

"It was really magnificent, beyond all expectation. The mirror, too, gave it back instantly; it was too convincing. It would not have been at all necessary to move much; this apparition was perfect, even though it did nothing. But I wanted to discover what I actually was, so I turned round a little and finally raised both arms: large gestures, as if in the act of exorcism, were, I saw immediately, the only fitting ones. But just at this solemn moment, I heard quite near me, muffled by my disguise, a mixed and very complicated noise. Much frightened, I lost sight of the presence in the mirror and I was grievously disturbed to perceive that I had over-turned a small round table laden with objects that were probably very fragile, though what they were Heaven alone knew. I bent down as well as I could, and found my worst fears confirmed: everything seemed to be in pieces. Two useless parrots of greenish-violet porcelain were of course shattered, each in a different, but equally malign, fashion. A box, from which rolled bonbons that looked like insects in silken chrysalids, had cast its cover a considerable distance away; only half of it was to be seen, the other half had quite disappeared. But most annoying of all, a scent-bottle had been shivered into a thousand tiny fragments, and from it there had been spilled some sort of old essence that now left a mark of very repulsive physiognomy on the spotless parquet. I wiped it up quickly with some of the stuff hanging about me, but it only became blacker and more unpleasant. I was, indeed, desperate. I picked myself up and tried to find something with which to repair the damage. But nothing was to be found. Besides I was so hampered, not only in my vision, but in my every movement, that my wrath rose against my absurd situation, which I no longer understood. I pulled at all the knots of my accoutrement; but that only made them tighter. The cords of the mantle were strangling me, and the stuff on my head was pressing down as though more and more were being added to it. Furthermore, the atmosphere had become heavy and as though mouldy with the stale odour of the spilled liquid.

"Hot and angry, I rushed to the mirror and watched with difficulty through the mask the working of my hands. But just for this the mirror had been waiting. Its moment of revenge had come. While I strove with measureless increasing anguish to tear myself somehow out of my dis-guise, it forced me, by what means I know not, to lift my eyes, and im-posed on me an image, nay, a reality, an alien, unbelievable, monstrous reality, with which, against my will, I became permeated: for now it was the stronger, and it was I who was the mirror. I stared at this great, terri-fying, unknown personage before me, and it seemed appalling to me that I should be alone with him. But at the very moment I thought thus, the worst befell: I lost all knowledge of myself, I simply ceased to exist. For one second I had an unutterable, sad, and futile longing for myself, then there was only he—there was nothing but he.

"I ran away from him, but now it was he that ran. He knocked against everything, he did not know the house, he had no idea where to go; he managed to get down a stair; he stumbled over someone in the passage who shouted in struggling free. A door opened, and several persons came out. Oh, oh, what a relief it was to recognise them! There were Sieversen, the good Sieversen, and the housemaid and the butler; now everything would be put right. But they did not spring forward to the rescue; their cruelty knew no bounds. They stood there and laughed; my God, they could stand there and laugh! I wept, but the mask did not let the tears escape; they ran down inside over my cheeks and dried at once, and ran and dried again. And at last I knelt before them, as no one has ever knelt before; I knelt, and lifted up my hands, and implored them, 'Take me out, if it is still possible, and keep hold of me!' But they did not hear; I had no longer any voice.

"Sierversen used to tell to the day of her death, how I sank down and how they went on laughing, thinking it was part of the play. They were used to that kind of thing from me. But then I had continued to lie there and never answered a word. And their fright when they finally discovered that I had fainted, and lay prostrate in all those clothes, like a bundle of something, just like a bundle."[2]

Rilke's narrative genius is better able to describe the situation of living behind masks than any purely rational analysis. If we transfer his description of a single experience on to the entire canvas of life, we get an insight into the disordered world that turns corruption into "experience". The search for security is changed to insecurity. The urge towards self-realization turns into the loss of the self. There is only one way out of this situation.

Life in Responsibility

The attitude described above (loss of self in the search for self) can be changed by a personal decision; by men beginning to respond to

2. R. M. Rilke, *Die Aufzeichnungen des Malte Laurids Brigge*, Leipzig, 1931, pp. 127 ff (Eng. trans.: *The Notebooks of Malte Laurids Brigge*, London, 1930).

other men in their concreteness. Man finds he can and may respond to happiness. He feels called to self-surrender. To the extent to which he completely empties himself and does not seek to own anything, he is able to share in the riches of a personal relationship. Even the unhappiness of strangers moves him inwardly. Slowly a new level of existence grows up around him. He experiences with increasing certainty the frailty of life, and how little he can accomplish by himself alone. So he tries to be available for simple service to his brother, day by day. He tries to find ways to be helpful, to give advice when the other does not know where to turn.

Thus a new world of values and obligations comes into existence for him. In order to help, he must be able to see the whole picture, to understand the problems at their root. And so there develops a system of responsibilities, a sphere of norms and laws. In order not to waste his energies, lacking choice and goal, in vanquishing the world, he sets up norms of behaviour, laws of response, well tried ways of behaviour. And in this clearly delineated, responsible world, he can act creatively, can carry a stranger's life with him, can be effectively "there" for others. Life itself contains new meaning for him, when it is seen in a firmly established framework.

It is of course true that he can test for himself all insights, norms and concepts which he employs for coming to terms with the world of responsibility. But the problem solves itself in that he is placed from the start in a cultural, linguistic and conceptual world that has been handed down to him, whose function it is to give him the tools he needs for mastering his destiny. These are in the form of already imprinted schemes of thought, feeling, behaviour and values that have already been explored by the community. A series of values and priorities, an entire world of symbolic images to explain the universe, a system of "must" and "must not"—all these are ready to hand. They canalize, guide and organize the energies of individual requirement. Thus man can live.

In taking up his life as a task to be performed, and in recognizing its demands as binding upon himself, a man acquires firm anchorage.

He is no longer subject to capricious and ephemeral moods. Perhaps he is not even in doubt that it is good to subject himself to the accepted order and there to test the love of his heart. But disappointment sets in. It is a disappointment with life itself. And at this point men cease to be available to others.

Life as Message

Here we come to man's ultimate search, the search for meaning and therefore, at bottom, the search for God. Not of course for a God of concepts but a God of his own life. For man to be lifted out of the narrowness of his existence, he must have discovered how frail life is before God. Wordless, waiting for an answer, man looks into the "terra incognita" of true being. His questions constantly return to statements which contain the two words in the human language that are most relevant to life—"Why" and "I".

Man stands there defenceless, alone with his God. No one, no man and no Church, no friend and no world view, can help him here. Nothing any longer stands between him and the eternal "Other". Hidden from us are the answers man receives from his God, perhaps in the form of silence. Each man will receive, though not perhaps till death, an eternally unique answer from God, an answer that relates exclusively to the shape of his own being. But even earlier man can have a profound knowledge of the meaning of life. Perhaps this knowledge cannot be formulated. But man can nevertheless say with an ultimate certainty: It is good. Everything has meaning. No one is lost for God.

Whoever says such things must not be questioned for reasons and proofs. Nor must we judge him according to our own principles. It is not perhaps a "truth" for us that he is speaking. It is a truth for him alone. As if God had called the whole of creation into being, for the sole reason of enabling this one man to hear his answer. And in a profound sense this is true. This man is now God's only creature. God's richness is such that he can totally give himself to every man, can be there only for him. And likewise for a second man, and a third, for millions and thousands of millions. That is the mystery of his infinity and inexhaustible richness.

A man, who has known himself in this way as the unique receptacle of God, will return to his fellow-men simply and humbly. He will meet his brother and his sister with courtesy and modesty. He will help them with infinite patience so that they too can find the way to God. His language will not be stirring. Perhaps he will have no new ideas, no new plans for conquering the world. His real effectiveness will lie elsewhere—in letting God shine through him; in the quiet joy of his life, and perhaps also in the resignation with which he knows about the strangeness of all things human, and accepts this strangeness. He will be present with a quiet readiness to reconcile superficial contradictions. And if he is unable to do so, he will be ready to listen, to understand, to share the sufferings and wretchedness of others, to undergo their experience.

What finally remains? Perhaps only an ultimate endeavour to seek for God. Or uprightness and openness before the Absolute. The Gospel describes this "ultimate" of life as follows:

Life as "daring"

We are told how Jesus walked upon the waters. In him there shone the joy of a God-seeking life. After the feeding of the 5,000, Jesus went up into the hills in order to pray by himself. He sent the disciples in the boat to the other side of the lake. The boat, while still far distant from land, was rocked by waves, for there was a contrary wind. Then Jesus came to them, walking on the sea. When the disciples saw him, they cried out, "It is a ghost!" They screamed in fear. But Jesus told them at once, "Take heart, it is I; have no fear." Here the story begins in earnest. Peter takes courage and calls out to him, "Lord, if it is you, bid me come to you on the water." And Jesus said to him, "Come." Then Peter summons up his entire courage to leave the boat and with it his friends, which were the then entire church: "So Peter got out of the boat and walked on the water and came to Jesus; but when he saw the wind, he was afraid, and beginning to sink he cried out, 'Lord, save me.' Jesus immediately reached out his hand and caught him, saying to him, 'Oh man of little faith, why did you doubt?' And when they got into the boat, the wind ceased" (Mt. 14. 22–32).

In this story we can see four elements of man's search for God—the appearing of God, the daring of man, salvation through God and the sending back into the community. Let us try to examine these four elements a little.

(a) *The appearing of God.* Peter was a sinner. He had denied Christ three times. Sin is "being far away" and "not being able to break through" to real nearness. It is something joyless, uncaring and self-seeking. It is life that is tired and hopeless. Christ has come to free us from all this. Man must throw himself into God's arms with the last of his powers, break away from his small world, his despair and confusion. Peter committed the sin of his life when he said of Jesus: "I do not know this man of whom you speak." But he pulled himself together at once. "And he broke down and wept" (Mk. 14. 66–72). To understand his courage one must realize that in the depths of his soul Peter was a coward. Yet it was to him that God appeared. Christ had left the disciples alone in the boat. And they got into desperate straits. Contrary winds blew towards them. The waves beat against the boat. At this point they saw a figure walking on the water. This did not lessen their terror. They did not recognize Jesus but cried out in fear—"A ghost." We can see from this that it is possible for God to come to us and we to take him for an apparition, unreal and without enduring entity. Perhaps Christians have only one task in the world—to show men by their life that total despair does not exist, that men can go on hoping, perhaps against all hope. It is difficult to believe that God became man for sinners, for the oppressed and down-trodden; for men who admit, in moments of truthfulness, that they are lost. To accept such a God is truly to "dare".

(b) *Man's daring*. At Jesus' words, Peter stepped on to the water. The depth of the water and his uncertainty are matters of basic human experience. Dangerous creatures live in the water. Man is afraid of them. But essentially his fear means that he cannot believe that limitless love and ultimate security exist. But now Jesus stands before Peter—a man who realized his life by being nothing but understanding and goodness, who was great above all in this, that he entered into all the limitations of life. He helped the sick, did not break the bent reed, did not extinguish the flickering flame. In him God's goodness and mercy appeared in our midst. The promise came from him: "I have set before you an open door, which no one is able to shut" (Rev. 3. 8). Because of this promise, Peter manages to overcome his fear of the waters.

(c) *Rescue by God*. Peter called out to Jesus. He probably did not clearly know who Jesus was. Only after the Resurrection were his eyes opened. But he knew that he could not live without him. So he said to this man—Let me come to you over the water. I no longer know who I am and who you are. Only one thing do I know with certainty, that you will never leave me. For you have said to us, "God is greater than our hearts, and he knows everything" (1 John 3. 20). All my thinking leads me to know one thing—that you are merciful, and I am a sinner. It is my very helplessness that makes me your friend. Your faithfulness is above everything in my life. In your goodness I am forever secure. Everything depends on whether I say the words—You, my Jesus, whoever you are, be merciful to me. But the waves and the tempest soon distract Peter from this self-surrender. Fear once again takes over. And he begins to sink. But fortunately Jesus is very near. Peter is able to stretch out his arms, seize the saving hand and raise himself up. He has doubted for a moment, but his God stood by him.

(d) *The sending back into the community*. Peter has felt the power of God. He has had his personal experience of God, outside concepts, formulas and systems. This experience had been the most inward element in his life.

But his God also wanted to be the God of his brother. It is like a slow and silent birth of the image of God in the soul of man. What did Jesus want to effect in us? Wherever man experiences the "God of his life"; wherever he finds him hidden in the depths of his soul, there he also finds the direction of his life. There he knows he has not been abandoned. He knows too that with all his false and mistaken starts, he is standing on firm ground. Wherever God overwhelms the innermost soul of man with his presence, there man acquires greater depth and humanity. There new ways are opened out to him to give him enough strength for at least the next few steps. Now man understands—Christ has not saved him from suffering but only from despair. For he said, "I am with you always." This was the meaning and purpose of Peter's lonely experience of Christ. His God was to be a revelation of God to his brothers.

Innumerable people live today in God's presence. We must be like these modest and humble people, in whom God's presence becomes his experienced nearness. In this way we shall experience anew, gratefully and humbly, in quiet concentration, the "God of our life" and our "first love of him". At the end of these meditations, we must leave the last word to God's mercy. It is a mercy that appeared to us in Jesus Christ, the friend of all the oppressed. Should your brother and sister need our advice, we can only say to them: "Do not speak much of your experience. But if someone near you is in need, then tell it him." Our God did not promise us an easy life. That is not the meaning of his message. But one thing he has promised to us all—that we shall be able to find him even amidst the greatest difficulties of our life; or at least shall meet a man who understands us. Our faith is a task laid upon us in the world. We are surrounded by the ordinary, everyday world. God has placed us in its midst. It is our life's work.